STUPID SEX

Also by Kathryn and Ross Petras

The 776 Stupidest Things Ever Said
The 776 Even Stupider Things Ever Said
The 776 Nastiest Things Ever Said
The 176 Stupidest Things Ever Done

STUPID SEX

The Most Idiotic and Embarrassing Intimate Encounters of All Time

Kathryn and Ross Petras

Broadway Books
New York

BROADWAY

A hardcover edition of this book was originally published in 1998 by Doubleday. It is here reprinted by arrangement with Doubleday.

Broadway Books titles may be purchased for business or promotional use or for special sales. For information, please write to: Special Markets Department, Random House, Inc., 1540 Broadway, New York, NY 10036.

BROADWAY BOOKS and its logo, a letter B bisected on the diagonal, are trademarks of Broadway Books, a division of Random House, Inc.

Visit our website at www.broadwaybooks.com

First Broadway Books trade paperback edition published 2001.

Designed by Carol Malcolm Russo / Signet M Design, Inc.

The Library of Congress Cataloging-in-Publication Data has cataloged the hardcover as:
Petras, Kathryn.
Stupid sex / Kathryn and Ross Petras. — 1st ed.
p.   cm.
"Main Street books."
1. Sex—Anecdotes.   2. Sex—Humor.
I. Petras, Ross.   II. Title.
HQ25.P47   1998
306.7—dc21   98-3266
                            CIP

ISBN 0-385-48851-3

10   9   8   7   6   5

Note

This book is a collection of humorous new articles gleaned from a variety of sources. Neither the author nor publisher accept any responsibility for the accuracy of the articles. All of the names used in the original articles have been changed; therefore, any resemblance to actual persons, living or dead, is purely coincidental.

Introduction

The position is undignified, the pleasure momentary,
and the consequences utterly damnable.

—LORD CHESTERFIELD ON SEX

Lord Chesterfield, that famous old bore, might have had a point. Not necessarily about regular sex, but about stupid sex—the sex acts that make you wonder about the general IQ levels of the human race.

What exactly is stupid sex? It's hard to define, but as the Supreme Court once said about pornography, you know it when you see it.

How else would you define the act of inserting a penis into a bowling ball? Or the idea of having sex *with*—not in—the family car? Or having sex in an airliner bathroom . . . and then getting so stuck the door has to be pried off—while several hundred fellow passengers watch with interest?

There are literally thousands of people out there having sex in the most undignified ways possible and with the most damnable consequences imaginable. And *Stupid Sex* has collected their stories.

It's a walk on the wild side of stupidity—a compendium of the most absurd, the most inane, and the most ridiculous *true* examples of stupid sex and ludicrous lewd behavior. Stories about sex itself and stories about the accessories of sex, stories about the consequences of sex, stories about *stories* about sex . . .

More specifically, *Stupid Sex* includes all of the different ways you can indulge in stupid sex and lewd behavior, like:

- Surprise Sex—a sexual variation on a surprise birthday party that usually goes terribly awry.

- Case of Mistaken Identity Sex—someone decides to surprise someone else with a fun, spontaneous sexual encounter . . . but winds up getting surprised him or herself. This often happens to newlyweds, people on vacations, and those who have trouble seeing.

- Technological Terror Sex—a consequence of the Information Age, this is sex that becomes stupid because of the misuse of any number of technological devices, like answering machines, automatic phone dialers, or homemade computerized gadgets.

- Wrong Place at the Wrong Time Sex—sex that goes astray just because you happen to be on top of a cliff, stuck in a sports car, or in a massage parlor that's being raided.

- Strange Spot Sex—when *where* the sex takes place is what makes it stupid. This often happens to people who are indulging in a little solo action, although it's also fairly common with people who are having a little fun on the side . . . and don't want their mate to know.

- Masturbation Madness—a catch-all type of stupid sex that typically involves a man and some sort of device—from pool nozzles to sink drains to vacuum cleaners.

- Big Business Meets Sex—the bizarre consequences when money and sex interact.

- The Strange Interaction Between Government and Sex—stupid sex laws, communist sex, and odd legal maneuvering.

It's also about topless garages, unusual uses for spermicidal gel, and enema bandits. And, of course, it's about the rugged individualists who ask the time-honored question: "What would happen if I stuck *it* into *this* inanimate object?" And finally it's about those who go it alone with the help of a mechanical pal— like a Veg-O-Matic or (but this is purely speculation) a trusty bovine electro-ejaculator.

They're all in here—from the foolish fetishes to the ridiculous rendezvous. It's a potpourri of the most preposterous sexual encounters ever.

Enjoy.

STUPID SEX

On Adultery, Proving

A sales manager in Johannesburg, South Africa, definitely suspected his wife of adultery. But he needed proof to get a divorce.

So one day he came home from work very early and hid in the attic above their bedroom, waiting for his wife and her alleged lover to arrive.

Sure enough, at just the right hour, he heard his wife enter the bedroom—with a man. And, sure enough, very soon he could hear the sounds of passionate lovemaking.

The manager was so busy listening he didn't notice that he too was making noise. But his wife and her lover did. Hearing funny scratching sounds in the ceiling, they called the police.

The police managed to get into the attic from the outside of the house, where they found the husband. But because of the combined weight of the husband and the cop, the ceiling collapsed.

And then, in the words of the happy husband, "Since we both

fell on the bed where my wife was having intercourse with her cousin Denis, I was able to substantiate my allegation."

The divorce was granted.

On Aquatic Self-Stimulation, Pool-Nozzle Style

An operator at 911 received a phone call at 4:45 one morning from a desk clerk at a Florida motel. One of the guests was stuck in the swimming pool. When the 911 operator asked how, the clerk paused. It was kind of hard to explain . . .

The police zipped to the scene and were greeted by the sight of a swimming pool with toilet paper floating around—and a guest, thirty-three-year-old Stephen Dumond, half underwater. Upon closer examination, Officer Mel Johnson noticed that Dumond's pants were down to his knees and his penis was stuck in a suction hole in the pool wall. "Under no circumstances contact my wife!" Dumond started screaming, at the same time trying to pull himself out.

But nothing budged. The cops shut off the pump, but Dumond had gotten so swollen in his attempts at escape that he was completely stuck. Finally they had to call the underwater paramedics. They poured lubricant around the suction fitting and, after two hours of work, were able to free the fun-seeking Dumond—who still had an eighteen-foot piece of pipe stuck on his groin.

The cops initially intended to prosecute him, but, as Officer Johnson put it: "There's no law covering unlawful sexual intercourse with a rubber chlorinator nozzle. But I'd still like to know what the toilet paper was all about."

So apparently did the press. Dumond was swamped by reporters when he left the medical center—but he was unrepentant.

"I can't see what all the fuss is about," he said. "It's the sort of accident that could happen to anyone."

On Artistic Ego, Problems with

A famous Austrian cartoonist was having an affair with a married woman. On a whim, he decided to draw a little cartoon on her buttocks—and, as he always did with his drawings, he signed it.

But the woman forgot to wash it off and later, when she undressed in front of her husband, her husband saw the cartoon, recognized the cartoonist's signature—and filed a criminal complaint against him.

On Autoeroticism, Family Car and

It was perhaps the first known case of *literal* autoeroticism. According to the journal of the Institute of Psychiatry, a man got into a hot and heavy sexual relationship with the family car.

Apparently his family belonged to a strict religious sect that banned any sex or even talk about sex before marriage, so like many young men, he went car-crazy. But he took it a little further than most people.

The young man would masturbate near the car tailpipe (whether he attempted penetration is unknown) and even put "erotic" snapshots of the car in his room.

Psychiatrists tried to reprogram him toward nonautomobile females and were partly successful—but the man's first love is still the car.

On Automatic Phone Dialing, Fun with

A mother in Devizes, England, was awakened out of a sound sleep early in the morning by the telephone. When she picked it up, all she heard were moans and groans. She assumed it was a prank call, hung up, and went back to sleep.

But a little later the phone rang again. And again the woman picked up the phone. But this time, instead of moans and groans, she heard shrieking and a woman screaming, "Oh, my God!" Her blood ran cold when she realized that she knew the voice—it was her daughter, who lived by herself a good hundred miles away. And she was obviously in trouble.

The mother quickly called the police, who immediately sent two cars to the daughter's house. They battered down the front door and ran inside, searching for the victim. And they found her . . .

Nude, in her bedroom, having sex with her boyfriend.

Apparently, in the act of making love, her toe had hit the

automatic dial button for her mother's number on the bedside phone.

A police spokesman had the definitive final word: "This is a warning for other people. If you're going to indulge in that sort of thing, move the phone."

On Bachelorette Parties, Extremely Surprising

It was the night before Amanda Grable's wedding—and her female friends were throwing her a party at a local disco.

The party really took off when the male stripper who had been hired by the sister of the bride danced in. Dressed as the Lone Ranger, complete with mask, he started bumping and grinding. "Take it off!" the women kept shouting—and he began stripping down to a polka-dot jockstrap.

"Take it off!" they kept screaming, none louder than the bride-to-be herself.

But it wasn't until he turned around to wiggle his ass in the women's faces that the bride-to-be *really* started to scream.

There, on the right cheek, was a tattoo of a skunk—a tattoo that was very familiar to her.

It belonged to her husband-to-be, who, up until that moment, she had thought was just a quiet, retiring trainee accountant.

On Balls, Bequested

A lord from Scotland was outraged when the Royal Bank of Scotland refused to allow him to withdraw a million pounds from his trust funds.

He decided to take action—and rewrote his will, including a very special bequest to the bank.

As he put it: "I'm leaving my balls to the Royal Bank . . . because that lot certainly haven't got any . . . The bank will get the entire scrotum, to put it in a nutshell."

The bank was not amused. A spokesman said, "The bequest is not appropriate . . . We are a [regular] bank, not a sperm bank."

On Baseball, the Real Attraction

A couple staying at the Skydome Hotel, visible from inside Toronto's baseball stadium, turned out to be the highlight of a Blue Jays–Seattle Mariners game back in the early 1990s.

When the couple made love during the game, several thousand fans saw every move. In an earlier incident, a man allegedly masturbated at the window, apparently thinking that the windows were made of one-way glass. Several thousand fans saw his every move too.

In the words of the hotel manager: "There isn't a more exciting way to watch a baseball game, but for some people it's more exciting than for others."

On Bathrobes, Pesky Easy-Opening

Apparently you just can't trust a bathrobe.

At least that's what a Portland, Oregon, man kept saying when he was admitted to a hospital emergency room with severe bruising and lacerations on his penis and testicles. It was all his bathrobe's fault . . .

Getting caught in a handheld vacuum cleaner could have happened to anybody, he insisted. Really.

As he told the story, it was all very innocent. He was vacuuming with a handheld vacuum cleaner while wearing his bathrobe—with nothing on underneath. His robe suddenly flew open and he tripped. And he just happened to fall on the vacuum cleaner, which, of course, just happened to still be running.

"[The robe] always does that," he told doctors. "I keep meaning to rig up some kind of tie for it, but I never do. I guess I'll get around to it now."

On Beemers, Sex and

A thirty-five-year-old man from Erlangen, Germany, found the perfect spot for a little secluded sex with his girlfriend: the trunk of his BMW.

They spread a blanket inside the trunk, climbed inside, and started enthusiastically making love. Maybe it was a little too enthusiastic . . . because the trunk slammed shut.

And the nude couple was trapped inside.

Luckily, the man happened to have his handy cell phone with him and managed to call the police. The police thought it was a prank call and hung up. The man called again and he finally managed to convince officers to send over a patrol car. The police opened the trunk, then they advised the couple on bedrooms, hotel rooms, and other better places for sex.

On Bees, Politically Correct

If you want to avoid getting harangued by the politically correct police, take the "bees" out of "the birds and the bees."

That's the lesson learned by the Dutch government.

Concerned about the spread of AIDS, a Dutch government agency decided to run an ad campaign—and since it was a sensitive topic, they wanted to come up with something that was as inoffensive as possible.

So they started running a television commercial, a cartoon showing a lustful-looking bee—a bee who didn't care about his health, but wanted to pollinate any flower he found. As the cartoon showed the bee flying from flower to flower, a somber voice-over said: "There is a disease that spreads through sex . . ." And finally, as the narration goes on to explain AIDS, the oversexed bee drops dead.

It *seemed* inoffensive enough—but one special interest group thought it was totally unfair. To bees. So the Dutch Beekeepers League issued a formal protest, spelling it all out:

". . . Bees are *not* promiscuous. They do not carry AIDS. And they do not visit flowers for sex—but for nectar."

On Bell Ringing, Causes for

The unusual question before a Sicilian tribunal: Is it illegal to ring a church bell in the middle of the night to commemorate an act of sexual intercourse?

This question came to light when a sixty-one-year-old man from Messina had sex with his twenty-year-old girlfriend. He was so delighted with the event that he ran to a vacant church and began ringing the bell in celebration.

His wife was not quite as delighted. She filed a nuisance complaint against him for making the noise.

But the tribunal sided with the happy copulator and refused to penalize him.

On **B**elt **B**uckles, **B**all-**B**usting

In December 1987 a man appeared at a fire station in Bristol, England. He was holding a shopping bag filled with ice in front of him, and he seemed very upset.

"What's the problem?" the firemen asked.

The man mumbled, fumbled, and shuffled in embarrassment.

Finally the bag was opened and the truth came out. The man had a big brass belt buckle stuck on his penis. It had gotten stuck there during some sexual fun and games with his wife. After trying to pull, push, and tug it off for three hours, his wife finally convinced him to get help. So she and his son packed the now hugely swollen member in ice and drove him to the fire station.

Unfortunately, the firemen weren't able to do much and had to drive the man, his still-swelling penis, and the shiny buckle to the Bristol Royal Infirmary, where doctors were finally able to remove the buckle. The man begged for anonymity, for "obvious reasons."

On Big Breasts, U.S. Government Dislike of

The Bureau of Alcohol, Tobacco, and Firearms banned an Italian wine from being imported into the United States. The reason? On the wine labels was a nude woman with large luscious breasts.

So the Italian wine company changed the label. They put on a nude woman with very small breasts—and the bureau okayed the wine.

On Bigness

Sometimes you can have too much of a good thing.

A student in Orland Park, Illinois, may be one person who falls into this category. He was forced to take off his pants by school authorities—to prove that the large bulge in the front of his pants was not a drug stash.

It wasn't.

To make things worse, when explaining just what was going on to the angry mother of the well-endowed boy, a teacher indelicately said, "I don't know how to put this to you delicately, but have you ever heard of John Holmes?"

Whether she had or not, the mother was not amused—and sued the school for $225,000.

On Bingo, Sexual Dangers of

A seventy-three-year-old woman was an avid bingo player until a fateful evening in 1990—when the bingo board at the Catholic church where she was playing fell on top of her.

She then filed suit against the church, claiming that she had suffered about $90,000 worth of damages.

It wasn't the immediate physical injuries she suffered that were bothering her, she explained, but the strange aftermath. She discovered that, after the bingo board debacle, she was suddenly attracted to women. In addition, she started suffering from "spontaneous orgasms"—which had nothing to do with other women or even men.

The church's attorney, however, was quick to point out: "It is unexplained in modern medicine how a bump on the head can alter sexual orientation or cause recurring orgasms."

After about six years of back-and-forth arguments, the lawsuit was dismissed.

On Bondage, Problems with

A fifty-five-year-old Burbank man placed a personal ad in a local bondage and discipline magazine, seeking a session with another man. When he got an answer to the ad, he set up a date at his own home.

The doorbell rang, and his date stood there. In line with the man's wishes to be dominated, the date immediately took charge—forcing the Burbank man to crawl through the house to his "bondage room," strip, and allow himself to be tied, nude, to an examining table.

Then the date had his own fun.

He left the man tied up in the room and, with an accomplice, stole his sofa, leather chair, television set, and stereo.

On Breakups, Tough Reactions to

Some people have a tendency to overreact a bit when someone breaks up with them.

This was the case with a Thai construction worker in Bahrain. His wife left him, so, in a fit of remorse, he did what he thought he had to do.

He cut off his penis.

Luckily, some friends found him, packed up the penis, and took both it and the man to the hospital, where it was reattached again. Said the urologist who handled the case, "He is much better now, talking and smiling with friends."

On Breasts, Diverting

Like many of her compatriots, a leading Bulgarian actress was concerned about the terrible economic troubles her country was going through. So in November 1996 she came up with a brilliant idea to help matters: She would have a plaster cast made of her breasts—which she would allow to be displayed in the National Theater in Sofia.

She hoped this would help keep people's minds off the dismal economy.

As she put it: "It is a pity to focus everything on [budget problems] when there are such beautiful breasts around."

On Breasts, Fun Pranks with

California is a free and easy state, but in this case, it was too much. It started when a woman was reported jumping from table to table in a pizza parlor, boasting loudly how four years after giving birth she could still produce milk. To prove it, she'd make a mooing sound and then squirt a little milk.

When the police arrived, the woman proceeded to ask Sergeant John Pollar if he could still remember the taste of mother's milk. When Pollar said he couldn't, she started squirting milk in his face.

Police later discovered the woman had a history of unauthorized milk squirting, including one incident at a national park where she squirted milk at a man with a baby, shouting, "Bet *you* can't do this, sonny!"

On Broadcast Nudes

Back in 1969 in the desert resort town of Palm Springs, California, viewers of local station KPLM were pleasantly surprised (or not so pleasantly surprised, depending on their viewpoint) when the late-night show ended and a nude couple suddenly appeared on the screen. Sure enough, they started making passionate—and very X-rated—love.

The station was deluged with phone calls. Police rushed to the broadcasting station—expecting to see the obvious. But nothing unusual was going on. Just the normal routine. The police didn't understand it.

They waited until the next night—and, sure enough, the same nude couple appeared on the screen doing their hot and heavy thing. Again the station was deluged with calls, and again the police rushed to the station, and again they found nothing.

This went on for a few nights more, as more and more people tuned in to watch. In most cases they weren't watching for pleasure, of course, but only as a painful civic duty to make sure that public morals weren't being corrupted.

And every night that same and by now quite familiar couple went on doing their thing. Finally police, concerned citizens, and TV people figured out what was going on. A broadcasting technician at the TV station had been watching a porno video to kill a few hours—and hadn't realized he was hooked up to broadcast.

Embarrassed managers of the TV station promised to rectify matters and earnestly hoped that "Our future service in the desert community will erase the memory of this deplorable incident."

On Buffets, Welsh

When the sculpture committee of the Welsh arts council went to a lunch, they found a buffet table that was a little bit different.

The food containers were made from casts of a nude female body.

In the words of the proud sculptor: "My breasts did for the soup bowls and my tummy for the plates. Later I added a casserole, which was formed around a cast of my behind. I do not feel the least embarrassed by having people eat off my body—so to speak. I am completely detached. I got the idea during a dinner party. All at once I realized what a marvelous food container the body is."

On Bulges, Incriminating

Sometimes it's best to be humble. This is what Marcus Rogers learned. According to a 1992 report in *Arab News* newspaper, Rogers was walking through an airport, loudly boasting about his sexual prowess. To prove his point about how irresistible he was, he pointed to the large bulge in his jeans.

It was large. Maybe too large.

Two security officials grew suspicious, pulled him aside, and had him searched.

The bulge turned out to be a fake penis stuffed with cocaine.

On Bull Terriers

It was Nigel Barnes's wedding day, the happiest day in his life. The fifty-nine-year-old Londoner lent his camcorder to a friend so the ceremony could be captured on tape. This way he could be sure he'd always remember this day.

He was right.

At the wedding reception, Barnes announced that he'd play the tape so the guests who hadn't been in church could see him and his wife exchanging vows. He popped the tape in the VCR, hit the play button, and leaned back . . .

And the shocked wedding guests were stunned to see video of the groom having sex with a dog.

Barnes had forgotten to erase the tape that had been used—a tape that included scenes of him getting it on with his neighbor's bull terrier, Ronnie.

He wound up in court—accused of cruelty to animals. And he

was defensive. The sex acts were simulated, he said. He was just trying something creative with trick photography. But the jury that heard his case thought the excuse was the only creative thing about the incident and convicted him.

On Bumper Stickers, Misread

A man in Santa Clara, California, was arrested for displaying lewd and pornographic material on his van.

It was all a mistake, the man claimed. For example, police misinterpreted one of his bumper stickers.

As he explained, it actually read: SUCK MY DUCK.

On Bureaucratic Views of Sex

According to certain people in Michigan, the poor may not get much money, but they get a lot of sex.

At least, that's what Michigan officials explained as their reasons for cutting back on free condom distribution.

According to a public health manager, Michigan cut back on condoms when they found that "The poor were selling their free condoms to teenagers at all-night parties. It will be a bad thing. Studies show that the poor have sex up to twenty times a day. There will be more and more of them."

On Canned Foods, Protected

It was enough to make a grown man gag.

The man from Newport, Tennessee, won a lawsuit against a major canned food company because he found a condom in his pork and beans.

According to his testimony, he had gone on a lunch break with some of his coworkers when he opened the can of beans and discovered the little surprise inside. He claimed that he became physically ill when he fished it out. And furthermore, the rubber made him the butt of jokes among his fellow employees.

It also made him $2,500 richer—the amount awarded by the jury.

On Cell Phones, the Bottom Line On

Doctors in trauma wards see a fair amount of strange things. But this was possibly the first time anyone had come in with a cell phone stuck up his butt—let alone a cell phone that kept ringing.

It happened in Los Angeles. An attorney was admitted into a trauma ward with a cell phone stuck up his ass. As he told the doctors, it was all his dog's fault.

The dog had always loved the phone. And this particular day he had dragged the phone into the shower while the attorney was showering. Somehow he slipped on the tile, tripped on the dog—and sat down right on the cell phone.

To make matters worse, somehow the cell phone cover opened when he plopped down on it. So the attorney was stuck with a cell phone that was *working* crammed up his ass.

The doctors couldn't stop laughing—especially when the phone rang three times during the three-hour extraction process.

As one doctor said: "By the time we finished, we really did expect to find an answering machine in there."

On Chaperones, Multitalented

Brian Mallon, a nurse, was accused of having sex with a woman in a swimming pool—a woman whom he had only met moments earlier. To make matters worse, he was having sex with her when he was supposed to have been supervising three mentally handicapped swimmers.

But Mallon had a ready excuse: The swimmers weren't "in any sense at risk because the act only took about half a minute." Besides, he argued, he had his eye on them the entire time.

On China, a Bad Place for a Little Porno Tape Viewing and

In 1990, in a crackdown on porn, Chinese communist officials announced two penalties for being in possession of pornography—life in prison or death.

On Chinese Antiporn Campaigns, Effectiveness of

The communist government of China decided to launch a public campaign against pornography under the slogan "Sweep the Yellow" in the 1980s. (Yellow is the color the Chinese associate with pornography.) The idea was for people to turn in all their pornography to the government.

But things immediately started getting out of hand. Thousands of people took the "yellow" part literally and turned in any books with yellow covers. Others turned in their nude baby pictures.

And others, eager to meet local quotas and to show how zealously antiporn they were, went out and bought pornography—and then turned it in. In fact, in many areas pornography sales actually increased.

On Closet Sex

A German housewife, in an effort to add zip to her matrimonial sex life, hid in the bedroom closet. When her husband entered the room, she sprang out.

Her surprised husband jumped back in terror, crashed through the bedroom door, and stumbled down the hall, tripping several more times and then hurtling out the hallway window.

On College, New Twists on Sex Ed. and

It's a long way from English 101. Students at the University of Rochester have a more unique course open to them, courtesy of the English department: "Alien Sex: Gender and Difference in Old and New Fantasy."

Lectures include one on "Metal Lovers," which incorporates a look at a Johnny Depp film, *Edward Scissorhands,* and assignments include watching *Dracula, Big, The Crying Game,* and *Star Trek.*

In addition, this highly educational course answers such probing questions as: "Do gods, demons, incubi, succubi, androids, and androgynes really offer a different sexuality or rather a way to 'cross-dress' the sameness of human experience?"

For an answer to this question, you'll have to take the course.

On College, New Twists on Sex Ed. and, Part II

Students in Berkeley's "Female Sexuality" course have a number of different enlightening assignments they can complete for credit.

Among them: completing a coloring book of female genitalia. And for the more enterprising: examining yourself with a speculum, a medical instrument designed to view the vagina and cervix. This last one, however, is an optional assignment—presumably open to women only.

On Come-Ons, Dangerous

A delivery man in Salt Lake City, Utah, was leaving an apartment building when he looked up and saw a beautiful nude woman waving alluringly at him.

Not one to overlook such a tempting invitation, he started to climb the fire escape of the apartment to meet his new amour, but she started to scream. So he came up the normal route and knocked on her door. By then, however, she had called the police, who nabbed him.

It turned out she had been waving alluringly to her boyfriend—who had just left the building.

On Commemorative Banners, Sex-Educational

The Martin Luther King, Jr., Library was opening up in San Jose in the Philippines. To commemorate the occasion, the city had a nine-meter-high banner strung up—embroidered with goodwill messages in twenty-seven different languages.

But only a few minutes before the minister of culture arrived for the opening ceremonies, the San Jose chief of police rushed up and ordered the banner torn down.

He had noticed something wrong with it at the last minute. The message written on the banner in Tagalog, the local language, read: ALWAYS USE A DOUBLE-STRENGTH CONDOM.

On Communist Ideals, Still Living

Slovakian communist leader Karcag Olomon—who proudly served communism as the sports officer for the regional Communist Party—found a new way to "serve the people" once the communists had been booted out of office.

Olomon opened a peep show: Happy House Peeps. As he proudly explained, his happy house isn't just your standard peep-and-run operation, but offers erotic massage, rooms for couples, and a vast library of porno books and tapes.

But Olomon's greatest joy, and one that he shares with his coworkers at Happy House Peeps, is that they are all "performing a useful public service." After all, he points out, "regular entertainment makes for a happy society."

Just read your Karl Marx.

On Condoms, Incriminating

Nineteen-year-old Bobby O'Fallon of Dublin, Ireland, was in court—charged with stealing two Durex condoms from an unattended car.

Down the hall, in another courtroom, was his girlfriend, Bernadette Neeson. Her crime? According to the literal-minded prosecutor, she had received stolen goods . . . in this case, the condoms.

On Contraception and the Army

Not many people would think that contraceptives have anything to do with national defense—but a Wisconsin state senator would disagree. There's a definite link between the strength of the Army and the availability of birth control.

In the early 1970s, the Wisconsin State Senate was holding

hearings on whether or not to repeal the state's restrictive birth control law.

But as one state senator testified, he was firmly against any repeal—not on moral grounds, but because of national security. He began by pointing out that the Vietnam War had been mainly fought by poorer people, then moved in for the clincher:

"Now you want to give contraceptives to poor people. Where are we going to get men for the armed forces if we have another conflict? It's a good way to destroy an army."

On Contraceptive Gel, Tempting

A woman in West Africa stored her contraceptive gel in the refrigerator because she was afraid that in the high heat prevailing in the tropical region it would melt.

One night, while giving a formal dinner party, she watched as the cook brought out the dessert of the evening. It was a large sherry trifle with cream, cherries, nuts—and topped off with a lovely glaze of contraceptive gel.

On Cornflakes, Little-Known Advantages of

Dr. John Kellogg, of Kellogg's cereal fame, championed dry breakfast cereals as an antidote to masturbation and other nasty sexual urges. His brother went on to sell the famous Kellogg's Corn Flakes—but today the Kellogg's company doesn't emphasize this interesting little factoid about their company's origins.

On Cracker Jack Prizes, Unique

Cracker Jack is a time-honored snack food, known for its surprise prize inside, like a fake diamond ring or a little puzzle book.

But in the late 1980s, an eight-year-old girl from Huntington, West Virginia, got a *really* surprising prize. She opened her Cracker Jack box and found a little booklet, about an inch square. Its title? *Erotic Sexual Positions from Around the World.*

Inside were several pages with explicit line drawings of people engaging in a number of interesting sex acts and positions.

According to the girl's grandmother, the girl's eyes got very big when she saw the surprise. But all was well.

The child thought it was an exercise book.

On Crimes, Genital

An herbal doctor from Nigeria had concocted the perfect crime: He would cheerfully walk down the street, walk up to people, shake their hands . . . then suddenly fall to the ground, screaming that his penis had disappeared.

The shocked victims would then be mugged by his colleagues.

The police finally caught up with him and came up with an unusual way of combatting his crime: They forced him to walk through town with his genitals exposed to prove that he was actually perfectly intact. In fact, he had fathered 114 children, many of whom were his accomplices.

On Damned If You Do, Damned If You Don't

A police officer from the vice squad in San Antonio, Texas, walked into a pornographic bookstore and arrested an ex-con for selling "lewd material."

"But you guys sent me here," the ex-con said.

"Tell that one to the judge."

So the ex-con explained to the judge that when he had gotten out of jail, his parole officer had sent him to the Texas Employment Commission, which in turn had sent him to the porno store for a job.

The judge dismissed the charges.

On Date Stamping, Advantages of

It had been a rocky day in a divorce court in a small town during the 1960s, back in the stricter days when you had to *prove* grounds for divorce.

The husband had been arguing against the divorce, but the wife was adamant. Why, she said, they hadn't even made love for at least eighteen months, maybe longer.

It was a lie, her husband declared angrily. They had made love just the other day on the floor of his office.

"He's lying!" shouted the wife. "It's been years."

Her lawyer smiled triumphantly. Lack of sexual affection was strong grounds for divorce.

"But I can prove it," the man said. "I definitely can prove it."

The court looked at him expectantly. How?

The man smiled. "I marked her ass with the office date stamp."

The divorce was denied.

On Dates, New Places to Find

A man from Wauwatosa, Wisconsin, was issued a citation for disorderly conduct in 1995—when he was found in the women's rest room at the Mayfair Mall.

He had a credible explanation for being there, though.

He told the police that he thought it would be a good place to meet women.

On Deep Questions, Why Not to Answer

Did you ever wonder if your penis—or someone else's—could fit in the hole in a barbell weight?

Someone in Wichita, Kansas, evidently did. Emergency room workers were surprised to see a man enter the ward with a large barbell weight stuck to his penis. Apparently the man had been pondering whether or not his penis would fit, so he decided to try. The problem was that it did fit—but once it became erect, it wouldn't fit back out again. The local fire department spent over twelve hours with bolt cutters, trying to pry the penis loose.

Finally a urologist was called in to drain blood from his engorged—and weighty—member.

On Department Store Sex

California police arrested a flasher in a department store in maybe the only case of "victimless flashing."

The man was flashing store mannequins. According to police, he not only flashed them, he fondled them, peered up their dresses, and in general molested them.

One police officer said of the unusual crime, "This is the first of a series of none, I hope."

On Descriptions, Not-so-Useful

People in Anchorage, Alaska, complained to the police that a man was exposing himself in public.

But the police had a problem finding the criminal. When asked to describe the man, everyone said they didn't get a good look at his face. What did they all notice? "An unusually large penis."

On Doing It for Your Country

The police in Honolulu, Hawaii, had one of those ideas that make you wonder about IQ levels at headquarters. They decided to pay money to private citizens to go and have sex with prostitutes—in return for testifying against them in court.

One local hotel manager promptly volunteered for the job out of (in his own words) "civic pride." He served his beloved city by getting reimbursed for $70 worth of sex with a prostitute in his car.

On Doing It for Your Queen and Canada

The police in Edmonton, Canada, also decided the best way to nab prostitutes was to pay local citizens to have sex with them.

The police paid over $600 to the brother of a fellow officer to go to a massage parlor for oral and regular sex. In another case, a local DA praised another private citizen who volunteered to go to prostitutes for his "marvelous sense of public duty."

On Dolphorama Shows, Highlights of

The highlight of the *Dolphorama* show in England in the 1970s was the part when the dolphins swam up to female swimmers and took off their bikinis.

Getting the dolphins to learn the trick was easy, *Dolphorama* officials explained. All they had to do was line the bikinis with fish meal and the dolphins enthusiastically stripped the women. The only problem—getting the women used to the dolphin's "touch."

The solution: They got an ex-naval officer from an underwater demolition squad to remove his false teeth and swim up to the women and use his lips to take off the bikinis.

It worked like a charm, and the shows went on without a hitch.

On Dresses, Revealing

Was the cause of the accident the dress—or the driver? This question was put before the court in Athens, Greece.

Apparently Katerina Hajidakis had boarded the Athens bus with a torn dress, torn in such a way as to arouse the interest of her fellow (male) passengers. So interested were they that they formed a crowd in the aisles, which prompted an argument from an elderly passenger who, far from promoting decent behavior, wanted a better shot of the woman and her torn dress.

All this in turn prompted the bus driver to periodically turn and yell at the passengers to sit back down. Not that he was completely innocent. Apparently he managed to sneak a few peeks himself. During one of these moments of staring behind rather than ahead, the road turned, but the bus didn't and it crashed into a cemetery, injuring fourteen passengers.

So whose fault was it? The passengers blamed the woman with the torn dress. The judge, a bit more civilized, blamed the driver and the passengers, not the woman.

The men promised to appeal.

On Drinks, Not-so-Refreshing

A Nebraska man left two thermos bottles in the back of his truck when he went to check into a motel. When he went back to his truck the next morning, he noticed that the thermoses were missing. Apparently a thirsty thief had walked off with them.

However, as he told the police when he reported the theft, he felt sorry for the thief if he decided to take a swig from the thermoses.

He owned a cattle-breeding business. And the two thermoses were filled with $3,275 worth of bull semen.

On Ducks, Penile-Loving

A jealous Thai woman was angry at her playboy husband. So she attacked him with scissors and snipped off his penis—and threw it out the window. The man rushed to the window—only to see a duck waddling off with his penis in its mouth.

On Electro-Ejaculators

It's not every day that someone's electro-ejaculator is stolen—but it happened at Michigan State University in 1991.

School officials reported that the $1,200 electric device used in artificial insemination for animals had been stolen from the school's veterinary clinic—for unknown, hopefully animal-related reasons.

On Enema Bandits

The notorious "enema bandit" of Urbana, Illinois, was finally caught and imprisoned—but not on the charges you might expect. The obsessive enema lover, a thirty-year-old man, would sneak up on unsuspecting people and administer enemas to them under gunpoint.

But the problem the arresting police officers had was that

there was no law on the books for unauthorized enema giving. Fortunately, during several enema sessions, the enema bandit had stolen some money from his victims, so he was charged with thievery.

On Erections, Remote-Control

It was the answer to an impotent man's dream. In 1992 a California man received an experimental electronic implant that would enable him to have an erection by remote control. Whenever he wanted to have sex, he could push a button and get a little lift.

There was one minor problem. The remote control device was so wonderfully sensitive that whenever a neighbor would use his remote control to raise his garage door, something else would go up along with it.

On Everything the Army Wants to Know About You and Isn't Afraid to Ask

Congress has put a stop to a polygraph test that the Pentagon used which asked questions that didn't seem to have much to do with national security.

Some questions the Army wants to know:

- Have you ever received sexual stimulation in a crowded area?

- Have you engaged in sex acts with an animal?

One person wondered why the animal question asks if you've ever engaged in sex acts, in the plural. Does the Army feel that one time with an animal doesn't count? The Army had no comment.

On Excuses, Weak

It was a clear case of "If you're caught in a tough spot, punt."

The police raided an Irish brothel—and found John Callahan lying naked on a sofa—in what the police described "a state of sexual arousal."

It was all a mistake, Callahan claimed. He was completely innocent of soliciting sex. In fact, he had no idea he was in a brothel.

"I was brought here by my friends to receive treatment for a football injury," he explained nervously. "Really."

On Exhibitionism, the Bottom Line on

Tucson, Arizona, residents were being terrorized by an exhibitionist in 1977. But not your ordinary, run-of-the-mill exhibitionist. This man would pop up outside people's living room windows wearing only a pair of underwear.

On his head.

On Explicit Love Letters, Why You Should Burn

Giovanni Vitale, an eighty-five-year-old Sicilian, found a very passionate, explicit love letter written to his wife.

Raging with jealousy, he stabbed his wife in the shoulder.

Unfortunately, he then found out that he had written the letter—fifty years earlier.

On Exposing Yourself, Legal Definitions of

In Nevada a man was arrested for exposing himself to a woman on the ski slopes. But the man didn't want to plead guilty, and the woman wanted to avoid a long trial, so local law officials came up with a compromise.

The man was asked to plead guilty to another charge. He agreed, the woman agreed, and so did the prosecutor—because, as he said: "In a way, it kind of fits the facts." The new charge?

Carrying a concealed weapon.

On Exposing Yourself, Simple Excuses for

John Thompson, a science lecturer from Cambridge, Massachusetts, was accused of indecent exposure by one of his students. But, as he later explained in court, it was all a simple misunderstanding . . .

"My wife's washing machine was defective in the rinse cycle and the soap powder in my underpants caused a rash on my genitals. This made them itch. So I started letting them hang out of my briefs. Unfortunately, during a tutorial with Marianne Baxter, I caught a whiff of her perfume, which caused my penis to become erect and, even more unfortunately, I had unwittingly left open my fly. My erection protruded through my lab coat and here I am.

"Incidentally," he added, "we have now purchased a new washing machine."

He was cleared of all charges.

On Factory Machines, Sex and

A man entered the hospital with a scrotum "twice the size of melon," according to the doctor on duty.

The man finally admitted this was due to his habit of taking a midafternoon masturbation break, using the canvas drive belt of a factory machine as a sort of industrial-size vibrator.

Unfortunately, the last time he tried it, one of his testicles got caught in the belt and was ripped off as the man was sent flying across the room. Seeing the damage but too embarrassed to report to the hospital, the man at first tried a little doctoring of his own—using an industrial stapler to close the wound with huge one-inch staples.

The man assured the doctor he was swearing off industrial-strength masturbation forever and said he would buy a sex doll for future midafternoon sessions.

On Family Ties, Loose

Police in Hermiston, Oregon, were called to a bar—on a complaint of public indecency.

When they arrived, they found a woman . . . wearing only kneesocks. And she was about to leave with four very drunk men.

The cops moved in to arrest all five, but the men protested. They weren't taking advantage of the woman. They were her family, taking her home. More specifically, they explained, they were, respectively, the woman's husband, brother, cousin, and uncle.

There was one problem with their story: None of them knew her name.

On Feeling Hot and Bothered

A man in Moscow walked into the medical clinic with a large, red, sore, swollen penis.

The cause? Not a disease, but the old hot pepper in the condom trick.

Apparently the Russian's wife decided to get a little revenge on her philandering husband, so she carefully unsealed the condoms in his pocket, doused them with hot pepper juice, and then carefully resealed them.

On Fertility Treatments, Dubious

In a certain central African country, a man was getting suspicious of the activities of his wife at the local fertility clinic.

So the next day he decided to sneak after her. He watched as she went inside the clinic and closed the door. Sneaking up to the door, the husband peeked through the keyhole and, sure enough, his wife was writhing in sexual passion on the floor with the fertility doctor.

The husband barged in and started screaming. But the doctor remained calm—even when the husband called the police.

The couple had wanted fertility treatments, right? As the doctor later explained in his defense in court: "I was giving his wife the last doses of pregnancy medicine for the day."

Besides, he explained, he never even charged for his services unless pregnancy resulted.

On Fire Risks, Sex and

It seemed like a fun idea at the time. One night in 1990, after a lot of drinking, an English woman allowed her boyfriend to paint her nude body with yacht varnish. As the perfect accessory to her new high-gloss look, she put on a dog collar as he requested.

The next morning it didn't seem like such a fun idea—especially when the woman discovered that she couldn't scrub the varnish off. Still extremely shiny (and still wearing the dog collar), she went to a local hospital emergency room for help. But when the doctors asked just how this whole thing had happened, she got embarrassed—and left without treatment.

Worried about her flammability, the doctors called the police—who finally were able to locate her and return her to the hospital, where the varnish was finally removed.

On Flashers, How to Identify

The police in Vancouver, British Columbia, were interviewing a woman who had rushed in, saying that a man had exposed himself to her.

She explained that she was a house painter who had been touching up the exterior of a downtown hotel when the man came over and opened his coat—exposing his nude body.

"Were there any identifying characteristics?" the cops asked her.

"Yes," she said. "In fact, there might be an easy way to identify him." As she explained, "The only weapon I had was my paint roller. So I painted him bright orange from the top of his bald head down to, well, you know where."

Armed with that information, the cops went out and easily caught their man: He was the only drunken man they found that had a bright orange stripe down the front of his body.

On Flashing, Unbearable

A man jumped into the bear pit at the London Zoo, pulled down his pants, and flashed an audience of sixty children. Then he turned and tried to entice two huge Russian bears to dance with him.

The zookeepers were not amused. But neither were the bears. "They just walked away. They were disgusted," said the chief bear keeper.

On Fowl Play

Ergut Kamal, a Turkish poultry breeder, was in court. His crime? Stabbing his eighty-year-old neighbor sixty-five times.

Kamal had a good reason for his action. It was a matter of honor.

As he explained to the judge, he heard a chicken squawking, ran outside, and was horrified to discover his neighbor raping his favorite chicken. And, if that wasn't bad enough, "he was even doing it in front of her baby chicks."

On **G**arbage **C**an **L**iners, **L**ittle-**K**nown **A**ppeal of

England is known for its eccentrics, but solicitor Jonathan Butler went too far when he was arrested for having sex with a public garbage can liner. Butler claimed it was the only way he could be sexually fulfilled.

According to his lawyer, who urged the judge to be merciful, Butler "has been prowling the streets at night, and the police have often surprised him in wheelie bins, and even in the backs of [garbage trucks]. In fact, his absolute sexual fantasy is to be in back of a [garbage truck], naked, when the bin bags are crushed.

The judge sentenced Butler to probation, and his girlfriend vowed to stand by her man . . . as long as he didn't help her put out the garbage.

On Gays, Increase in

Prison officials in Dade County, Florida, began housing gay males in the women's prison in the early 1980s. It was part of a humane effort to reduce sexual abuse and overcrowding at the men's jail.

But the prison officials began to notice something surprising. The number of men declaring themselves to be gay was increasing rapidly.

The women's prison was cleaner, more pleasant, safer, and offered one distinct advantage—plenty of women.

On Getting Off, Peculiar Ways

A man from Ohio had a bang-up time when he masturbated . . . literally.

He would play with his penis until he had an erection. Then, when he was completely sexually aroused, he would shoot himself. With a gun.

But he wasn't completely crazy. He did wear a bulletproof vest.

On Getting Rid of Prostitution, Dangers of

The *Vallejo Times Herald* in Vallejo, California, launched a spirited campaign to get the police to clean up a local hotbed of prostitution. Police did their job, only to find that the prostitutes had relocated to a friendlier venue.

The new location? The parking lot of the *Vallejo Times Herald*. The prostitutes were conducting business in a camper parked between two newspaper trucks.

The reaction of the paper to the revelation was not reported.

On Getting Your Neighbor's Attention, Bad Ideas for

A Santa Cruz, California, man called the police with a complaint: His neighbor was driving him crazy. She just wouldn't leave him alone.

A police officer drove to the house to investigate. When he pulled up, he saw what appeared to be a live chocolate Easter Bunny hopping away from the man's house. It was the next-door neighbor—who had entirely covered her nude body with chocolate and bounced over to her neighbor's house, hoping to attract his attention.

After what the cop termed a "sticky struggle," she was arrested.

On Gum, Erotic

Is chewing gum part of a fiendish plot to destroy the morals of Egyptian virgins?

According to an Egyptian member of parliament, the answer is clearly yes.

"As soon as a girl chews this evil gum, she goes into a sexual fit and loses all self-control," he said in a 1996 speech. Why? As he explains: "This gum, which is called the Wrigley, is flavored with the notorious aphrodisiac spearmint—and it's well known in Israel for its erotic effects."

On Hair Salons, Topless

The owner of a men's hair salon in Adelaide, Australia, came up with what he thought was a brilliant idea to attract more business: topless hairdressing.

But then the president of South Australia's Hairdressers and Cosmetologists Employer's Association got wind of the idea and became upset that it "would degrade the whole industry."

As the president so cogently—and oddly—put it: "What would happen if the girls . . . spill some particular hair products on their nipples?"

Unfortunately, that burning question remains unanswered.

On Handcuff and Family Dog Sex

A couple in Fort Lauderdale, Florida, decided to add some spice to their sex life by using a pair of handcuffs. One of the members of the fun couple was handcuffed to the floor-to-ceiling bookcase in the bedroom. Then they both handcuffed themselves together. They were all set for a hot time, when the husband dropped the key. As he stretched to reach it, the family dog bounded over, curious to investigate what was going on, and snuffled the floor where the key lay. The husband tried desperately to pick up the key, but it was too late.

The dog swallowed it.

The nude couple was attached to the bookcase with no way to release themselves. They did, however, manage to reach the phone and call the police. And the police arrived to find them— still nude, still handcuffed, and very embarrassed. As they told Patrolman Fred Hansens, they were just "fooling around" when disaster struck.

"I feel like kicking the hell out of that dog," the man added.

On High-Level Sex

Politicians and top-level executives apparently really let their hair down in the bedroom—no matter how stuffy they are in public.

Consider this: Two psychiatrists interviewed forty-two expensive call girls and found that sixty percent of their clients were top-level government or corporate execs.

And both groups "overwhelmingly" asked for whipping, bondage, and humiliation services from the call girls. Eighty percent were married.

On High-Rise Rappelling Sex

"**H**ank" Chiang, a Hong Kong man who lived in a high-rise, was bored with his normal routine. Every night he would scan with his binoculars, searching for women undressing near the windows of their high-rise apartment building.

There had to be a better way . . . a more *close-up* way of sexual peeping.

Chiang finally hit on a brilliant plan . . .

He tied a rope from the top of the apartment building and rappelled down the side, peering into window after window until he finally stopped at the twelfth floor.

This was when a fifty-year-old woman, undressing in her

apartment on the twelfth floor, saw the most unusual sight: A naked man was dangling outside her window, carefully holding a rope with one hand and taking care of business with the other.

She screamed. Chiang, in a panic, tried to quickly rappel back to the roof, where he had left his clothes, but perhaps nervous from his unconsummated state, he slipped and fell.

Fortunately, he landed on the apartment entrance awning. He told the police he should have used a telescope instead.

On High-Security Sex

A female terrorist doing time in Italy's maximum security prison was found to be pregnant by a fellow terrorist.

An Italian government official commented, "This sort of thing makes nonsense of our claim that Italy's maximum security prisons are impregnable."

A prison official blamed the court system. "We feel sure she was fructified while she was in the dock."

On Hippos, Hapless

A pygmy hippopotamus at the San Francisco Zoo was bombing out when it came to mating. He had a mate—but he couldn't seem to figure out what to do with her.

According to a zoo official, Roly, the male, lived with his mate, Poly, since 1969. But all the mating efforts he made were doomed to failure.

As the official explained: "He'd put it in her ear, he'd put it under her arm. In twenty-six years he never put it in the right spot."

On Hobbies, Shocking

A seventy-nine-year-old amateur radio operator apparently got more of a charge out of his hobby than most people would have expected.

The sheriff's department of Zephyr Hills, Florida, found the man unconscious in his radio workshop, suffering from what the officials politely termed accidental electrical shock.

More specifically, the man had what the cops called an "unusual device" attached to his penis and connected to his radio transmitter by a voltage-controlling rheostat.

On Hogs, Horny

Harley-Davidson motorcycles are known as "hogs"—so maybe that's why a stray fifty-pound potbellied pig named Chi-Chi fell in love with one.

A woman in Key West, Florida, heard a noise and looked out her window. There she saw the pig trying to have sex with the front wheel of her husband's Harley. In his lustful frenzy, he scratched the paint, tore the bike's fabric cover, and, all in all, caused about $100 worth damage.

So Key West animal control officers said Chi-Chi would have to be neutered. But Chi-Chi had his defenders, including the motorcycle's owner, who pointed out that "his crime is an alleged sex act against a Harley. We don't even know if that's a felony!"

A developer raised cash for a "Spring Chi-Chi" defense fund; and the president of the Monroe County Bar Association was handling the case pro bono—free of charge.

As a final show of goodwill, the owner of a motorcycle dealership was considering giving Chi-Chi the run of his showroom for a night.

On Hoover Dustettes, Sexually Aggressive

It was all the fault of the vacuum cleaner, the sixty-year-old man claimed at the hospital.

While his wife was at the hospital, he "spontaneously" decided to vacuum the house in the nude. All of a sudden, while he was changing the plug of the Hoover Dustette, it "turned itself on" and caught his penis—tearing it and lacerating it in its frenzy.

Doctors sewed the lacerations with catgut.

On Hoover Dustettes, Sexually Aggressive, Part II

In another case involving a Hoover Dustette, a railway signalman was in his signal box when he bent over to pick up some tools. He somehow happened to catch his penis in a Hoover Dustette, "which happened to be switched on." Doctors repaired his injured member, also with catgut stitches.

On Hoover Dustettes, Sexually Aggressive (Probable)

In yet another case, a man was vacuuming his friend's house in a loose-fitting gown. He bent over to turn the machine off, when, all of a sudden, his "dressing gown became undone" and, according to the *Journal of Urology,* suddenly his "penis was sucked into the vacuum cleaner." The man sustained multiple lacerations, but his penis was well repaired with catgut. This time the make of the offending vacuum cleaner was not specified.

The urologists who reported these incidents in a distinguished medical journal dryly noted that these men were actually "probably in search of sexual excitement." Probably.

The journal went on to discuss the sexual features of the Hoover Dustette: It "has fan blades about fifteen centimeters from the inlet," It notes that "the patients may well have thought that the penis would be clear of the fan but were driven to new lengths by the novelty of the experience—and then came to grief."

On Hot Cops

Six official cars from the state of Connecticut were wrecked when a group of off-duty cops, guardians of law and order, jumped on them to get a better view of the participants at a wet T-shirt contest.

The police union agreed to pay for repairs.

On Hot Dogs

A policeman in Staffordshire, England, came home from the night shift one early morning in 1995 and saw his wife in the kitchen, making breakfast.

But the policeman was not in the mood for breakfast. Hoping to entice his wife into a little kitchen sex, the policeman thought up a very amusing little joke.

He pulled out his penis, wrapped it in a slice of bread, and offered the tempting morsel to his wife.

Unfortunately, his pet dog, a large Labrador, thought the "hot dog" was for him. He leaped over and took a quick hungry bite . . . and the man fell rolling to the floor.

Fortunately, a hospital was nearby, and top cosmetic surgeons repaired the damage. The policeman's friends at the station house were anxiously waiting to see how he filled out his medical claims form.

On Hotel Trysts, Slippery

In November 1989, an Army officer from Fort Leavenworth, Kansas, decided to show his wife his romantic, masculine, sexy side. He would *carry* her back to their hotel room, just like in the movies.

It seemed like a good romantic idea and it started out fine. But unfortunately, the officer's wife was wearing a fur coat that was kind of slippery . . .

As the macho officer tried to get a better grip, he tripped and fell forward—and his wife slipped out of his hands completely—hurtling over a three-foot-high wood railing.

Unfortunately, on the other side of the three-foot-high wood railing was an eight-floor drop into the hotel lobby—which the officer's wife soon realized as she plummeted down seventy-five feet. Fortunately, she landed on a restaurant table, smashing it completely, breaking her legs, but alive and well nonetheless.

On Impulse, Impulses Concerning

A thirty-nine-year-old married Wisconsin lawyer had settled in for an evening of fun, doing what he often did. But this night things didn't turn out right—and he was forced to go to the emergency room with a somewhat unique problem:

He had a bottle of Impulse Body Spray cologne stuck up his ass.

Apparently he had done this a number of times before. Normally he could pull the bottle right out. But not this time. He had tried desperately to remove the bottle, but even probing around with a handy back scratcher wouldn't get the Impulse loose.

As the doctor's report clinically stated: "Edema of the rectum and sigmoid colon precluded the successful manual removal of the object in the emergency room. A pelvic X-ray film showed the object to be lodged twelve centimeters proximal to the dentate line. The three-by seventeen-centimeter object, Impulse Body Spray, was removed manually after a spinal anesthetic. The patient was discharged on the second postoperative day. He refused psychologic counseling."

No word on how he explained his hospital stay to his wife.

On Incendiary Sex, Animal-Involving

"In retrospect, lighting the match was my big mistake."

So said Thomas Ericson to the fascinated doctors at the Severe Burns Unit at the Salt Lake City Hospital, where, along with his partner, he was being treated for burns.

So why had he lit a match? "I was only trying to retrieve the gerbil."

But let's start at the beginning . . . It all started when Ericson and his partner, "Ray" Selwyn, decided to have a little fun with their gerbil, Baggot. Ericson pushed a cardboard tube up Selwyn's anus and slipped the gerbil into the tube. A few seconds later Selwyn yelled out, "Armageddon!"—their "safe" word to let Ericson know he'd had enough. But apparently Baggot, the gerbil, hadn't. He wouldn't climb back down the tube.

Ericson tried looking into the tube, but it was too dark to see anything. Finally he had a bright idea: He lit a match, thinking the light might attract the gerbil.

But the match ignited a pocket of intestinal gas. The flame shot up the tube, ignited Ericson's mustache, and burned his face. As for Baggot, his fur was set on fire—which ignited an even *larger* pocket of gas farther up in the intestine. It set up such a charge that the gerbil became a furry, flaming cannonball—propelled out with incredible force.

The upshot? Selwyn wound up with first- and second-degree burns to his anus and lower intestinal tract; Ericson with second-degree burns to his face . . . plus a broken nose from the impact of the gerbil.

On Indecent Exposures

The Hillsborough County, Florida, sheriff's office received a troubling phone call from a woman. Apparently a young man, identified by the caller as Tommy Miltiades, had exposed himself to a four-year-old girl during a family picnic.

The police immediately called the Miltiades family. And

a woman who said she was Tommy's mother answered the phone.

The deputy first explained that someone had accused Tommy of indecent exposure. To demonstrate the severity of the charge, he explained the penalty—fifteen years in prison. Then he asked if he could speak with Tommy in person.

The mother paused for a moment.

It would be a little tough, she explained. Her son was *there,* all right, but he couldn't speak to the police. He couldn't speak to anyone, actually. In fact, he couldn't speak at *all.*

The reason? He was only thirteen months old.

On the IRS, Attitudes Toward Sex

In the late 1960s, the all-seeing IRS began to crack down on prostitutes. They put their crack accountants to work, carefully scrutinizing the tax returns of women convicted of prostitution.

Was this part of an antivice program with federal law enforcement officers to put the heat on sex crimes?

No, of course not.

"We're not out to control vice—that's a police problem," an IRS official explained tersely. "We just want them to file their returns and pay their taxes."

On Jail Beds, Alluring

A man from Texarkana, Arkansas, was arrested on charges of being drunk in public.

The man proceeded to make matters much worse by getting his penis stuck in his metal jail bed. Apparently he saw a hole in the bed and couldn't resist sticking it in. Jailers tried to ease his penis out, but instead it swelled up like a big red balloon.

Jailers were forced to disconnect the bed from the wall with a blowtorch, and the man, his penis, and the bed finished their time in a nearby hospital.

On Jail Breaks, Why to Remain Celibate During

It was a perfectly planned jail break. Eight inmates of the metropolitan jail in Nashville, Tennessee, kidnapped one of their guards and overpowered another. Then, free from their cells, they made their way to the women's jail.

Once they got there, they decided to indulge in what they'd been missing and have a little sex.

It had been a long time. And the sex was good—so good, in fact, that they decided to go at it a little more . . . and a little more . . .

Unfortunately, they were having such a great time—and making so much noise—that the other jail guards, armed with shotguns, were able to find them and recapture them.

On Japanese Products, Unexpected Sexy Names and

Matsushita Electric Industrial Company of Japan was introducing a new home computer product line under its Panasonic brand in Japan. And it came up with the catchy brand name Woody—as in woodpecker.

Then it came up with a new niche product in the line—PCs that had touch-screen capability—and the company came up with the clever name Touch Woody.

Last but not least came the utility to download Internet home pages—dubbed Internet Pecker.

It wasn't until an American worker at the company heard the names that top management realized that these products might not quite have the right sales appeal in American markets.

On Jeopardy, Italian-Style

An audience-participation quiz show is a real hit on Italian television—but it's also drawing a lot of protest.

On the show the contestants are all women—and if they fail to answer a question correctly before viewers call in the right answer, they take off one piece of clothing at a time.

The questions keep getting harder, and viewers stay up late at night, following the questions carefully and trying to get the women to strip completely.

As you'd expect, feminist and religious groups are against the show completely—but so are certain corporations. The reason? The day after the show airs absenteeism is up and productivity is down.

On Jobs, Dangerous

An assistant DA in Huntsville, Alabama, was just doing his job—collecting evidence to close a local adult movie theater. After watching fourteen films as evidence, however, he had to bow out of the police raid and instead was sent to the local emergency ward.

The diagnosis: temporary acute high blood pressure.

On Jobs, Ones to Avoid

In one of the more unpleasant careers of the universe, a certain worker in the Maryland Health Department is dispatched each day to the local sewage plant.

Apparently the Maryland Health Department wants to estimate how many people are practicing safe sex.

So the worker's job is to fish out and count used condoms in the sewage.

On the Joy of Sects

A Taiwanese man has founded the Penis Worship Sect, which promotes the belief that self-awareness can only be attained by focusing one's mind on one's penis.

The sect is not sexist, because, as its founder explains, "The woman's penis is in the breasts, which have enough strength to lift one thousand kilograms if harnessed properly."

Interestingly, once "penis power" is harnessed properly, the male or female penis can "walk, talk, even sing on its own."

The founder of the religion did note, rather sadly, however, that "few people who have the courage to declare in public that they worship penises."

On Judges, Overly Horny

In Taiwan a man named Li Peng was under arrest for embezzlement. The case was coming up for trial.

The judge in the case, meeting Li Peng's wife for a pretrial session, had a bright idea. He offered to make a deal. If she'd fork over a little up front money and have a little sex with him, he'd let her husband off.

Mrs. Li agreed. She and the judge went together to a hotel room. She closed the door. The eager and happy judge ripped off his pants—and then Mrs. Li promptly took his pants and ran.

She brought them later to the judge's own trial—as evidence of corruption.

On Lap Dancing, Lewd or Not

The definition of "lewd behavior" all depends on who's being lewd to whom.

A lap dancer was arrested for "lewd behavior" in Key West, Florida, and presumably was heading for a conviction. But then her lawyer pointed out that the lap dancer had performed the same dances at a local policeman's bachelor party, and, in fact, policemen were regular customers at the place she performed.

By a pure coincidence, before things could go further, the Florida assistant district attorney suddenly asked for a mistrial.

On Last Words, Touching

A seventy-four-year-old poultry farmer was found dead at his African farm, surrounded by fourteen chickens, also dead.

As the police deduced, the man apparently had taken a lethal amount of an aphrodisiac called *mudanhatsindi,* vomited, then collapsed and died—and when the birds ate his vomit, they died as well.

A police inspector commented poetically on the case to reporters: "Poor man. He thought *mudanhatsindi* would make him as erect as the uppermost branch of a *yatza* tree. But now he is dead, and his cock will evermore be limp. And so shall his hens."

On Lawn Ornaments, Titillating

A farm in west-central Illinois had a very lifelike concrete buck and doe in the front yard.

How lifelike were they?

Apparently *very* lifelike. Enough to fool another deer.

A young lonely deer saw the two ornaments and charged the buck. Then, when the buck didn't challenge him, the deer figured all was okay. So he turned around and mounted the concrete doe.

When he was done, he turned his attention back to the male ornament. This time he didn't charge it. Instead, he made love to it too.

The farmer tried to scare the deer away, but the deer wouldn't go. He kept going at it, resting on the ground between each sexual act, then going back to the job at hand.

For three hours this continued, until a truck finally scared the deer away. The farmer noticed that the doe's tail had fallen off—but the buck remained intact.

On Legal Technicalities

A Vancouver nightclub was in trouble with the British Columbia Liquor Control Board due to the nude dance act it featured.

The owner learned that he had broken the law—not because he had nude dancers at his club, but because he didn't have an orchestra of at least three pieces.

More than willing to live up to the letter of the law, the nightclub owner hired three musicians to play while the nude dancers danced . . . three nude female musicians, to be exact.

It was just fine with the board. As one spokesman noted: "As long as he has three musicians, how they are attired is of no concern to us."

On Lewdness, Legal

What does "lewd" really mean?

A teacher in Salt Lake City, Utah, got a little dictionary lesson when he was mooned by the mother of a student he had kept after school.

The mother was arrested for lewd behavior. But a judge decided that since she had been wearing panties when the mooning occurred, it wasn't lewd. Lewd mooning, he determined, means that the cheeks must show.

On Losing It All

"This accident was bound to happen sooner or later," said a police spokesman in India.

It all began with Mohandas Gopal, a commuter who was riding a bus to work in a busy Indian city. Suddenly, out of the crowd on the bus, an overly ambitious pickpocket struck at Gopal with a knife—hoping to release Gopal's wallet from his front pocket.

Unfortunately, the overzealous pickpocket slashed just a little too hard and released some other items from Gopal's body as well . . .

A police spokesman, in what has to be the understatement of the year, said that Gopal was actually "in luck, because in the confusion his vital organs were dropped on the floor of the bus."

And so the "lucky" Gopal was able to pick up his penis and balls and have them sewn back on.

But as far as the police were concerned, the matter was far from over. They urged local citizens to "make underwear out of strong tin foil with haste. Yes, it is uncomfortable when you sit, but only with metal protection around you will your wallet and your genitals be safe."

On Love Is Blind

Love is blind, they say. And in some cases, it's blinder than in others. For Bruno McCauley, it was Seeing Eye dog time.

He was shocked when he discovered that his wife of three and a half years was actually a man.

He learned the amazing truth after his wife disappeared and he filed a missing persons report. The police found his "wife"—thirty-four-year-old Don Salvio, now traveling as a man with a beard—using stolen credit cards in Las Vegas, so they arrested him for credit card fraud.

McCauley was amazed. It had never dawned on him . . . He had met Salvio at the University of Utah Health Sciences Center, where Salvio (who, in preparation for a sex change operation, had his testicles removed, but not his penis) was masquerading as a female doctor, Donna.

McCauley was smitten. They had sex only once—but Donna claimed she was pregnant—with twins. So the conscientious McCauley immediately married her.

McCauley later explained that he never had a clue that Salvio wasn't a woman because the marriage had been a celibate one and Salvio never let McCauley see him naked. As for the supposed twins, Salvio had explained them away by saying they were stillborn.

Now McCauley was seeking an annulment on the grounds of

irreconcilable differences. His final comment on the situation: "I feel pretty stupid."

On Lube Businesses, New Twists on

A Des Moines, Iowa, man came up with a great way for drumming up extra business for his garage.

He realized that the key to beating out the competition was to come up with a service that none of the other area garages were offering.

So he came up with a variation on the standard lube job and watched his business grow over fifty percent in the first month alone.

The new service? He had topless women clean and vacuum the cars. And he named this innovation with a very catchy title: Boob and Lube.

Unfortunately, though, the new business didn't last too long. But it wasn't the fault of public pressure. According to the owner, the women workers "just weren't reliable enough."

On Maggots vs. Cobras

"**L**earn from my misfortunes . . . Last week I thought twelve centimeters was not enough to satisfy my wife. How will I satisfy her with *no* centimeters?"

These were the words of a Thai man who had fallen for a con—a fake penis enlargement treatment that a large number of men in Chiang Mai, Thailand, had heard about.

It sounded too good to be true—and, of course, it was. The con men would inject a "magic potion" (actually a mixture of olive oil, chalk, kapok, and pieces of the telephone directory) into the victim's penis—and the penis would immediately get larger. Unfortunately, that's because it was swelling from the injection. A few days later it would become extremely infected. And a few days after that it might even need amputation.

The hospital was getting flooded with men suffering the consequences of the treatment. And the doctor who had been treating the afflicted men issued the following statement in the local press, hoping to dissuade anyone who was still tempted:

"Remember that a happy maggot is better by far than a gorgeous king cobra."

On Mail Order, Problems with

Mrs. J. D. Rollins, aged ninety-one, was very, very upset. The good Australian lady had ordered a luminous statue of Jesus from a mail-order company. When the box came in the mail, she opened it and found, instead of Jesus, a nine-inch dildo wrapped in a copy of *Sexual Intercourse: The Full Facts*.

On Man's Best Friend

Staffers at a major New York City hospital couldn't help laughing when a patient appeared in the emergency ward—closely followed by a dog. Very closely followed.

In fact, the dog was attached to the man's butt. Staffers watched in disbelief as the two close friends, man and beast, slowly shuffled their way into the admitting room.

What had happened? As the very embarrassed man explained to doctors and nurses, the dog had been having sex with him, and all had been going fine until the dog's penis swelled and got trapped up his rectum. Both man and dog kept trying to free themselves, but to no avail.

The man and his pet were taken in and specialists worked to reduce the dog's swelling. How the man made it to the emergency room (via a bus, a taxi, or a private car) is unknown, but was the cause of many happy hours of speculation.

On Massages, Clerical

A number of priests in Turin, Italy, were arrested in the early 1970s at a massage parlor. The code words used to get in for a full-body massage were, appropriately enough, "peace and good-will."

One nude priest, arrested by vice squad members while in the clutches of a nude young woman, explained it was all part of his work: "I needed the experience to understand the problems of my parishioners," he said.

On Masturbation, Those Annoying Clicks and

Some surgeons are a cut above.

These are the doctors that the annual All-Philippines Surgical Presentation Contest is designed to honor. And in 1990 one doctor won the top prize . . . for a great bit of surgical genius.

His patient appeared before the panel of judgments and made the following statement that put his doctor over the top:

"My firm belief in regular masturbation as a way to a trouble-free love life, and the fact that I have been masturbating for up to ten times a day for the last thirty years caused me to fracture my penis—a condition usually associated with bones, but in my case represented by a tear in the penile wall that resulted in a dramatic curve in my erection. This curve caused a clicking sound during masturbation, which ruined my ability to concentrate, and a debilitating softness of the organ."

Happily, the patient reported that his health was fully restored after the doctor operated on him. In fact, as he put it: "I was back to my regular performance."

On May Day Traditions, Little-Known

Lars Larson, a sixty-year-old employee, was fired from his job at a major food company. The cause for his dismissal: gross misconduct.

To put it more specifically, he put his penis in the ear of one of his coworkers.

But Larson had a ready excuse: All he did was "give Eric an eary," he explained. "It's traditional. It's part of our May Day celebrations."

On Medical Students, Dubious Pranks by

Hank Morse, a British medical student, decided to have a little fun. He removed a penis from one of the cadavers in the hospital dissection room, put it in his fly, and strolled along Westminster Bridge.

When people noticed the man parading along with an exposed penis, all hell broke loose. A police sergeant tried to arrest him for indecent exposure, but Morse pulled the penis free from his pants and threw it in the Thames with a cheerful: "There goes your f**king evidence!"

At this point, the policeman and three tourists who had been watching fainted dead away.

On Mile-High Sex, Hazards of

A couple on a flight from Athens to New York decided to join the mile-high club.

They went to the bathroom in the rear of the plane and proceeded to have delightful mile-high sex.

Unfortunately, they were both rather large people. And once their afternoon delight was over, they realized they had a problem. A big problem. They were stuck. They tried shifting positions, they tried sucking in their stomachs, they tried everything. They were still stuck.

Finally they did the inevitable. They started thumping on the bathroom door.

The airline was able to take care of their problem. But not before five technicians, countless passengers, the pilot, stewards, and stewardesses gaped as the nude couple was revealed, still coupling, so to speak, as the bathroom doors were removed.

On Moaning and Groaning, Legal

A thirty-two-year-old teacher from West Berlin was driving the other residents in her apartment building crazy. They kept waking up late at night, bothered by the incredible noise coming from her apartment. She kept ignoring their complaints, so they finally banded together and filed a formal complaint with the city court.

But even though the court agreed that the noise level was probably too high, the residents lost the case. The problem? Municipal antinoise regulations were pretty specific.

They didn't apply to the moans and groans a woman could make while having sex.

On Moral Power

The Moral Power Party of Thailand takes itself pretty seriously. Its leader actually abstains from sex with his wife on moral grounds.

So when the number-three man of the party, a certain Mr. Barnharm, turned out to be the producer of such movie hits as *Topless Heaven* and *Tokyo Teenager,* Moral Party members were not amused.

They were even less amused when it was discovered that Mr. Barnharm actually appeared in the movie himself, in a cameo role as a bra salesman.

As far as the Moral Power Party was concerned, that was it. He was kicked out.

But Barnharm didn't get the fuss. In fact, as he pointed out, his films "revealed an understanding of people's ordinary problems." And isn't that just what politicians should have?

On Motel Sex, Unexpected Dangers of

Couples at a motel in Venezuela were enjoying a little afternoon sex when the local "morality brigade" struck.

Armed with shotguns and rifles, morality brigade members raided the motel and tied up the owner, then they went from room to room, where they forced the couples to strip—at which point brigade members delivered a long lecture about virtue, chastity, and the advantages of virginity.

Then they left, leaving all money and valuables, but taking the guests' clothing.

The guests left later, wrapped in sheets.

On Murphy Bed Demonstrations, Necessity of Nudity for

Mr. Heinrich Horst of Germany was being sued for divorce by his wife on the grounds of adultery.

As she described it in court, she had seen it with her own eyes. She had walked into the bedroom and heard muffled cries coming from behind the panel of their wall bed. She pressed the release button and the bed came down with a thud—and Horst and their neighbor Inga Reiser bounced onto the floor, completely nude.

Horst had a ready explanation: It wasn't what it appeared to be. It was simply an accident. He had been showing Kraus how the wall bed worked when they suddenly got shut up in it.

The judge was not impressed with the defense. As he succinctly put it, "You do not have to be naked to demonstrate how a wall bed works."

On Night Watchmen, Interesting Moments on the Job for

It wasn't a normal night for one Botswanan night watchman. As he put it later, during court testimony, "It's not every day that you catch a naked man in flagrante delicto with a female donkey while doing your rounds."

It all started a little after midnight, when the watchman heard what he thought was the intermittent screeching of brakes, got a few of his coworkers, and ran to investigate.

When he shined his flashlight on the area the noise was coming from, instead of seeing a car, he saw a donkey—with a man balancing himself behind it on the curve of its legs.

The night watchman tried to talk him out of it. "Why do you want a donkey when there are so many women around?"

The man had a quick response: The women were all refusing him, the donkey didn't mind, and anyway it was his donkey and the night watchmen were just jealous.

On Nipples, Mandatorily Covered

In Lynnwood, Washington, where beefcake men were competing for that coveted title of Mr. Male, sharp observers might have noticed that not one male nipple was in sight.

All were covered by pasties or, in one case, by tiny American flags.

There was a reason for the covered male nipples. By a Lynnwood city ordinance, no humans may show their nipples in public. No mention is made whether the nipples in question are male or female. So to avoid antidiscrimination suits by women if men were allowed to show their nipples, city officials made sure the nipples ban stood.

They assigned three officers to the pageant—all detailed to keep a stern eye in sight for any uncovered male nipple.

On Nude Beaches, Problems at

A man was arrested for illegal public nudity at a French beach in Britanny. The police found him standing right among the organizers of the nude bathing day.

"But I'm innocent," the man furiously explained to the police. "I'm not with *them*."

Actually, he quickly explained, he was a member of a local *antinudist* group called Decency. And he had been sent to the beach as a spy. Of course, he had taken off his clothes to fit in.

And that was where his problems had all started. Walking along the beach, he had noticed four beautiful—and very nude—young women. They came up to him.

That was when the man had started to feel the pressure. Unlike a normal nudist, he couldn't take all this young feminine nudity physiologically in stride. In fact, a telltale symbol of his reaction to the nude young woman began to rise . . . and rise.

And it was the very public elevation of his penis that led him, the man explained anxiously, to approach the organizer of the nude festivities. He was actually asking him to point the way out of the nude bathing area—fast.

The police ended his unhappy erection by arresting him and fining him about $100.

On Nude Joggers, Tricky Disguises and

A man in Illinois was arrested for public indecency after the police caught him jogging in the nude. Just a routine arrest, except for one thing—the man had apparently been evading capture for a long time. Why hadn't the police caught the nude jogger before? At a distance, it looked like he was wearing jogging shorts.

Closer up, the police could see that he had used shoe polish to paint jogging shorts on his body. And even closer up, the police could see one telltale giveaway, of course, that paint couldn't hide.

On Nude Sunbathing, Dangers of

A woman in Durban, South Africa, was sunbathing on a rooftop in the nude when she heard someone yell out a sexual proposition. The noise seemed to be coming from above. She couldn't figure it out—until the proposition came again as a man in a hang glider swooped down by her once more, repeating his offer of sex a second time.

He didn't get a chance to make a third offer. An antiaircraft battery went into operation.

The woman's husband appeared on the roof with a rifle and attempted to shoot down the aerial propositioner.

On Nudity, Great Moments in Legislation About

In 1971 a Louisiana state senator discovered that the Louisiana State University yearbook contained photos of nudes—so he pushed for legislation that would legally prohibit nudity in classrooms, art studios, anywhere on the campus of the public university.

A fellow legislator pointed out that medical classes could pose a problem. After all, students worked on nude cadavers.

But the senator made his point perfectly clear: "A dead nude isn't as bad as a live nude. It's a *live* nude that causes temptations."

On Organs, Muscular

Qi gong is the ancient Chinese art of body control, developed by Taoist monks thousands of years ago. One modern master, who operates out of a studio in Hong Kong on Temple Street, practices and teaches the art with a difference:

He trains his penis to lift weights.

At a 1995 demonstration, Mo Ka Wang warmed up by swinging 100-pound weights with his penis, then for the final event, attached over 250 pounds of weights to his penis and lifted them over two feet off the ground.

Wang claims his training can cure impotence, premature ejaculation, and bed-wetting.

On Panties, Harassing

A woman named Mrs. Soo was defending herself in the North Singapore Court. Her alleged crime? She was accused of taking off her panties and waving them in the face of a Mrs. Wan.

But her attorney claimed that it wasn't Mrs. Soo's fault. In 1989, three years earlier, Mrs. Wan cut in front of Mrs. Soo on line at the Star Supermarket. Mrs. Soo complained, so an angry Mrs. Wan did the only logical thing she could to show her irritation: She took off her panties and waved them in Mrs. Soo's face.

According to the attorney, since then each time Mrs. Wan saw his client, she would reenact the crime: She would take off her panties and wave them at Mrs. Soo. "What can my client do in the face of this insult except remove her own in turn?" he asked the judge.

Unfortunately, there is no report of what the judge replied.

On Patio Furniture, Ball-Busting

Sitting outside in the nude can be dangerous. A man discovered this for himself when he decided to have a seat outside on a patio chair after taking a shower one fine summer day in Eastbourne, England. Unfortunately, when he tried to get up, he found he had an unusual problem. He couldn't. His balls were trapped between the slats of his patio chair. When the fire department arrived, the firemen rose to the occasion and tried all sorts of lubricants, but nothing worked. Finally the decision was made to cut apart the chair with a saw—very carefully.

On Peckers

Ronald O'Casey, a customs official at the Adelaide International Airport in Australia, noticed a man who was acting peculiar—he was limping, wincing in pain, and acting pretty odd in general.

O'Casey got more suspicious when he opened the man's suitcase and saw feathers and bird droppings. Then he heard noises coming from the man's pants and realized that something was definitely up.

He had the man strip—and found four rare Thai parrots, worth about $20,000, inside his underwear. His penis had been almost pecked off and his testicles were sweating profusely.

In court, the man swore he was as shocked as everyone else when the parrots were discovered inside his underwear. But finally he changed his plea to guilty and paid a steep fine.

As for the birds, they seemed no worse for the wear. O'Casey decided to keep them, but, as he told the judge, "Curiously, since their experience, they will only eat bananas."

On Peeping Toms, Leaving on the Lights and

Three renters in an apartment in Arizona successfully sued a next-door neighbor for invasion of privacy. They realized the neighbor had been spying on them in the shower via a two-way mirror in the bathroom.

Their clue? One night they turned the bathroom lights off—but the mirror stayed on.

On Penis Costumes vs. Vagina Costumes

A Venetian performance artist was arrested for dancing in a giant penis costume in the Piazza San Marco. The artist was surprised: "Last year I dressed up as a vagina and there was no trouble at all."

On Penises, Furry

A female government worker in Adelaide, Australia, and her husband, an office supervisor in the same department, filed claims against the department, saying both were made physically and mentally ill.

The woman received about $10,800 in rehabilitation expenses, including counseling, health club membership, and money to take an interior decorating course. Her husband won $34,000 in benefits for suffering anxiety and depression. But the woman's claim for sickness benefits was rejected.

What caused all of this anguish? A Christmas gift that a female colleague had received and displayed on her file cabinet—a furry penis.

On Penises, Metallic

A Malaysian man sued a prostitute for assault and theft in 1994.

In her defense, the prostitute said she became frightened when the man took off his clothes—because she saw the man's penis gleaming metallically in the dark.

It sounded far-fetched. But the prostitute wasn't lying. It turned out that the man had gone for a penis enlargement operation—and had had small ball bearings incompetently implanted in his penis by a doctor who, incidentally, turned out to be a fish-gutter.

On Penis Wars

Was it some sort of joke? Or an attempt to prove that South Korean men are a bit more virile . . . and much, much larger . . . than normal human beings?

No one really knows. But for some reason, five million South Korean condoms were sent to India—and the South Korean condoms were much, much longer and much, much wider than normal Indian condoms.

Enraged Indian doctors protested the mega-condoms at an official meeting of the World Health Organization in Bombay. According to one doctor, "As a medical man of thirty years, I tell you this is a sheath for a donkey, not a man."

Another Indian doctor said, "This is a revenge on the manhood of India." And, in fact, he added in a purely scientific and objective spirit, "It is well known that Korean gentlemen are more *petite* than average on all points south the navel."

On People Undergoing Sex Changes, How to Identify

In London, England, clever subway officials figured out a way to avoid confusion for ticket collectors who are faced with riders undergoing sex changes.

Instead of having only one identity card, these riders will be issued two—one for the rider as a woman; another for the rider as a man.

On Perverts, Sweet

In 1981 a woman was attacked in her Virginia Beach, Virginia, apartment.

She hadn't locked her door, so a man walked in while she was sleeping and made his way to her bedroom. He didn't tell her to take off her clothes and he didn't rape her. Instead, he forcibly covered her face and clothed body with chocolate and vanilla cake frosting—while telling her that she "should have known this would happen if you leave your doors unlocked."

A detective commented on the horrible scene: "She looked like Al Jolson. She was a mess."

On Phone Sex, Dangerous

For months, single men in Copenhagen, Denmark, had been getting phone messages that went something like this:

> *"Hey, sexy, I'm Inga, I'm a thirty-four-year-old stewardess with a hot body and I'm hot for you. So come on over to my house and show me your stuff."*

Helpfully, Inga would leave her address. Some people may have noticed that her voice sounded kind of quivery, but Inga explained in her message that she was so hot she couldn't even speak clearly.

And, sure enough, many young men rushed on over. Coming

to her house, each eager man would hear Inga's voice coming out from behind a window, ordering him to undress, so she could "judge him on his merits."

And each eager young man did just that. And then . . .

The reason for the quivery voice would become clear. It belonged, not to a thirty-four-year-old, but to someone almost three times the age.

Specifically, it belonged to gray-haired old lady, who would burst out from behind the window, shouting at the hapless naked young men, "Don't you know there's a ninety-two-year-old lady in the house." Then she'd threaten to call the police—unless the naked man would pay a $100 fine. She was backed up by a young strong-looking man—her son.

Most men paid up.

It wasn't a bad racket. Inga went through hundreds of men until someone told the police. The rest had been a little too embarrassed.

On Phone Sex, Politically Incorrect

Raven was a popular operator on a Nevada phone sex line. A long-haired, palomino-tanned, half-Cherokee beauty, she thrilled listeners with her hot sex talk.

But never in their wildest dreams did her many happy phone sex customers know the *real* Raven.

She was a burly twenty-nine-year-old ex-Marine with a wife and four kids.

Raven claims that the Nevada phone sex company fired him once they found out he wasn't who he says he was. In the spirit of the times, he's filing a suit against them—for sex discrimination.

On Police Officers, Extremely Conscientious

When it comes to catching people in the act of lewd or obscene behavior, it's uncanny just how careful and conscientious certain police officers become.

The first case in point: An undercover vice cop in San Francisco answered an ad in an underground paper that stated that, for a $70 modeling fee, a person could videotape a married couple in a range of sex acts. The officer paid up. The couple started having sex and the officer, mindful of his civic duty and clearly wanting to be completely sure that he had sewn up the case, waited. And watched. And videotaped. He did this for a full hour . . . *then* he arrested them.

But that's nothing when compared to vice squad detectives from Los Angeles. A local nightclub was apparently breaking the law by offering live nude dancers as entertainment. So the detectives went to see the show to determine exactly what charges to file. It apparently was very tough to decide . . . since the cops wound up watching the show seventy-five times.

Finally there was the vice squad in San Juan, Puerto Rico, who, in the early 1970s, came up with the perfect way of nailing prostitutes. To be sure they had evidence against them, the cops would have sex with the prostitutes and *then* arrest them. It was a surefire way of making sure the evidence stood up in court, they explained.

On Politics vs. Sex

During the height of the Cold War, a Soviet Aeroflot airliner landed in Ireland's Shannon Airport for a brief stopover, en route to Havana, Cuba.

A Russian man and a woman got off the plane and hesitantly approached a duty-free store counter at the airport. "Please help. I need protection," the man said in halting English.

The duty-free clerk quickly informed local authorities that a Russian couple was seeking to defect from communism—

and quickly, before the Soviet KGB could catch on, the police and immigration officials whisked the couple away to a safe place.

But during the initial interrogation, the police realized that it had all been a mistake. The man and woman didn't want *political* protection, but *sexual* protection—in other words, condoms.

In this area, the Irish police couldn't help—condoms could only be sold to married couples under prescription in Ireland at the time.

On Pool Toys, Fun with

A public pool supervisor noticed something a little suspicious going on in the children's pool. Two men were acting odd. One kept diving underwater over and over again, coming up for air, then diving back under. And all the time the other man wasn't moving a muscle.

As the supervisor later put it, one of the men was "strangely still and glassy-eyed. This is usually a sign that someone is urinating, and I was on the lookout for a telltale cloud of yellow."

The eagle-eyed pool supervisor moved in for a closer look. And instead of seeing that little cloud he expected to see, he realized that the diving man had a battery-powered toy shark and was rubbing it against the standing man's lower torso underwater.

That was enough for the pool supervisor to see. He began blowing on his whistle, ordered them out of the pool, lectured them on public hygiene, broke one of their arms, and called the police.

The men were each jailed for six months. And the pool supervisor had the final word. As he told reporters later: "Such behavior is disgraceful. It pollutes the minds of young people, not to say the water. If only such people controlled their urges, we wouldn't need to add so much chlorine."

On Pork Products, Part I

It's not all that often that luncheon meat figures in difficulties with sexual performance. But this is what happened in the Philippines in 1995.

As a worried man explained to the Philippine equivalent of

Ann Landers, the problem was that his wife worked in a meat-processing factory. And although she was clean and showered regularly, whenever they made love the smell of meat, mostly roast pork, predominated. The man went on to say, "I do not like the smell of meat as I enjoy penetration, and I would really like her to change her job, but she says that jobs are not easy to get. Is there a solution?"

The Philippine Ann Landers was not fazed. "Stuff two wads of cotton wool up your nose . . . and be grateful she does not work in a fish factory."

On Pork Products, Part II

A factory in Detroit, Michigan, manufactured an unusual dog food—made from pig penises. According to the president, "Dogs love 'em. I got the idea of making pig penises into pet treats around the time of the Lorena Bobbit trial. We were already using pig ears, hoofs, snouts, hearts, feet, and livers. So why not the pizzles?"

Why not indeed? Very soon, sales reached over $100,000 a month.

Then came the U.S. Agricultural Department. They demanded the company dye the pig penises green—to show they weren't fit for human consumption. The company president wasn't happy. After all, his pig penis product was clean and wholesome. "You could feed it to your kids," he said proudly.

And so his company started lobbying Congress to get the green penis issue overturned. And in the meantime, the company president threatened to import foreign—and undyed—pig penises. But as he somewhat cryptically said, "Who wants a foreign pig penis in their mouth? Don't answer that."

On Pork Products, Part III

A man was arrested in Reno, Nevada, for rape—after sexually assaulting someone with a pork sausage. The evidence had been destroyed, but police found remnants of the sausage in the defendant's pocket and the victim's underwear.

On Porn, Misleading

Hundreds of furious moviegoers trashed a local movie theater in Rio de Janeiro, Brazil. The movie that they had paid to see—*Furious Copulation*—was not what the title suggested. Instead, it showed a man chasing a chicken.

The owner promised to change the title on the marquee—to *The Pervert's Express.*

On Porno Films, Disappointing

The owner of the Tunnel of Love Sex Shop in Greenwich, England, was standing trial—not for the more normal charge of selling pornography, but for the unusual crime of selling things that weren't pornographic *enough.*

More specifically, a local couple, Mr. and Mrs. Chauncy Park, charged him with deception. He had sold them a Triple X video, but, upon viewing, it turned out to be a Chinese version of the eighties prime-time soap *Dynasty*.

On Pornographic Feminists

Two members of a group called Feminists Fighting Pornography were arrested in New York—for being pornographic.

It turned out the two women had a very graphic display, intended to show how porno degrades and offends women, set up on the sidewalk.

But then local residents complained that the pornographic pictures offended *them* and asked that they be removed. The women refused to take them down.

So police came and arrested the women—for third-degree obscenity and public display of pornographic sexual material.

On Porn Stars, Inadvertent

A newly married couple in Turin, Italy, set up a videocamera in their bedroom to tape all of their honeymoon activities.

But somehow, when they connected the camera to their tape machine, certain crucial wires got crossed.

So, as they were enjoying their honeymoon sex, so was anyone else in the apartment building who had turned their television set on.

The couple had accidentally connected the videocamera to the building's cable television system.

On Precociousness

You can't begin too early, at least according to the Katy school district in Texas.

First graders were issued a student conduct handbook that warned the 6 year olds they could be expelled for conduct such as "an act involving contact between the person's mouth or genitals and the anus or genitals of an animal or fowl."

On Pregnancy, Little-Known Reasons for

According to a 1975 study, Ankara has the second-highest birth-rate of any city in the world. And there's a good reason:

Jet airplanes and train whistles.

As the Family Planning Association of Eskiselir in western Turkey explained: "Awakened by the aircraft of the military base and the trains at the military station, our townspeople continue to respond too readily to the stirrings of nature."

On Products, Sexy

Used panties from high school girls are passé, explained a top official from a Japanese company specializing in satisfying the tastes of certain Japanese men. You can get used high school girl panties from vending machines, after all. The hot seller this year?

Fresh saliva, spit out by willing Japanese girls. "It's our store's number-one seller," the official explained. "No sooner do we put the bottles on the shelves than they are sold out, and our only fear is that supplies may dry up."

But to make certain current supplies stay wet, the company refrigerates the bottles (with a picture of the donor on the bottle) and guarantees the saliva is not more than ten days old.

According to the official, interviewed in the *Mainichi Daily News,* "It's now easier for the girls to sell their saliva than their panties and, if we can get regular supplies, we're planning to start bottling female high school student menstrual fluid next year."

On Prostitutes, Good Citizenship and

It seemed like an idea whose time had come: In 1973 the Idaho Department of Environmental and Community Services received a twenty-page staff proposal to train Idaho prostitutes as mental health counselors.

The prostitutes, once trained, could use their skills to counsel johns or, if necessary, refer them to other state agencies that could help them with their problem. As the proposal helpfully pointed out, this would be a great cost-saver to the taxpaying public "by providing assistance to the client through an agency already within the community, which is paid for through private enterprise."

The head of the agency was forced to turn down the innovative idea since prostitution was illegal—but he was "impressed with the employee's knowledge of the subject."

On Prostitution, Your AMEX Card and

Not many people go out of their way to *prove* they've been with prostitutes.

But that's what a man tried to do when he was told he owed $6,716.92 on his American Express card.

The man had a novel—but apparently legal—excuse for not paying. He told American Express he had used the money to pay for sex with prostitutes. And so, according to his lawyer, "a contract that has as its purpose an underlying illegality cannot be enforced by either of the parties." In other words, he shouldn't have to pay. The Maryland courts agreed.

On Public Bathrooms, Big Brother and

Police in Coeur d'Alene, Idaho, were being maybe just a little bit overzealous when they arrested a man for masturbating—in a closed toilet stall of a public rest room.

It turns out the police had drilled a hole in the wall of the stall and were peeping through to catch people engaged in sex.

The court ruled that people still have some right to privacy—including the right to go to the bathroom and masturbate, if the whim hits them, without the police on the other side, peering in.

On Quick-Change Artists

A man and a woman were looking forward to a quiet weekend in the country, but instead had to endure police loudspeakers, blaring sirens, and the chuffing of a police helicopter as it circled low over the woods near their house.

The problem? A French tourist had noticed a beautiful woman walking into the woods by the house. And then, maybe half an hour later, he had seen a shifty-looking man skulking out of the woods, carrying her dress and looking carefully to see if anybody had seen him.

The French tourist immediately notified the police. And the police were worried, very worried. Patrolmen were sent out, then the police helicopter. Finally, after hours of hovering and circling, the police got their man—and their woman too.

The man was a transvestite who had sneaked into the woods to change out of his dress before returning home to his wife.

On the Real Thing in Birth Control, Fascinating Facts About

While it's not recommended to use Coca-Cola as a spermicidal douche, the Harvard Medical School admits that they can't say it *doesn't* work.

In fact, in a series of in vitro tests, Coke was it—when it came to killing sperm.

More specifically, the results of their testing: New Coke killed the fewest sperm; Classic Coke had five times the effect; and Diet Coke was the strongest of all.

As a medical researcher put it: "Whether this was due to an extra 'fizz effect' or to the secret Coca-Cola formula we simply do not know."

On Reckless Driving, Good Reasons for

Police officers from Jefferson County, Missouri, found nineteen-year-old Frank Jones driving through a city councilman's rose garden—and charged him with reckless driving.

But Jones was quick to point out that he wasn't drunk and, in fact, had a very good reason for losing control of his car.

His girlfriend had accidentally bitten down while performing oral sex on him.

On Rectums, Interesting Things Found in

A number of odd objects had somehow found their way into rectums. In most cases, the person who had one of these objects in him explained it away by saying that the object "slipped in" by mistake or, of course, that he "sat by accident" on it. According to numerous doctors' reports, among the items that have been discovered are: a teacup, a shampoo bottle *and* bar of soap, a frozen pig's tail, a paperweight, a bottle of Mrs. Butterworth's syrup, a hard-boiled egg, a pair of reading glasses, *The Church Times* magazine, two bananas, a sand-filled inner tube from a bicycle tire, a turnip, a peanut butter jar, and five tangerines.

On Roadside Attractions

Traffic suddenly became bumper to bumper in one stretch of the major Italian highway that links many of Italy's largest cities. Police went to investigate.

They discovered that people were slowing down to gawk at a new roadside attraction:

Two nude people were having sex on the high-banked shoulder of the road. Not just plain vanilla sex; they were trying out a number of "interesting and unusual positions," as a police officer later reported.

Police interviewed the couple—and were especially shocked to discover that they had met only about fifteen minutes before their outdoor shenanigans.

It was all relatively simple, Hans Brunnah explained. The woman was hitchhiking to Rome and "as my wife was asleep in the back of the car, we decided to enjoy copulation in the open air."

On Rock 'n' Roll, Golden Nudie Tunes and

A group of expatriate rock musicians in Italy just weren't getting any gigs.

Finally they were approached by a promoter who offered them a deal—$500 for a one-night stint. There was one hitch. They had to appear in the nude. The promoter explained that this was only reasonable, since they were to perform for Southern Italy's largest nudist colony. And he wanted them to play famous "nudie hits" like *I'm in the Nude for Love, In the Nude,* and of course, that old favorite, *Sgt. Pepper's Lonely Nudist Band.*

The musicians weren't all that wild about the idea, but they needed the money, so they agreed.

The night of the performance they were taken to the auditorium and ordered to strip backstage. Taking off their clothes, they hesitantly walked on to the stage, with their guitars strategically placed—only to see a very surprised, very conservative middle-aged audience dressed in tuxedos and evening dress.

The audience was furious, the musicians were embarrassed, and the promoter was nowhere to be found. The musicians were even more upset by the banner announcing their rock group: THE NUDIE BLUES.

On Roosters, Gay

A New Mexico researcher tried an experiment to get hens to lay two eggs a day—and it worked. He gave the hens female hormones and their egg production went up.

But the hormones affected some of the roosters as well. He noted one rooster flirting with the other roosters, clucking, singing, looking coy, and acting "as female as he could."

On Royal Tributes, Excessive

It was May 1, the king of Thailand's birthday—his fifty-fifth, to be exact—and 719 of his male subjects decided to do the right thing to honor the day.

They all got vasectomized.

It's all part of Thailand's drive to keep the birthrate down. Each year the government offers free seven-minute vasectomies to any takers—in honor of the king.

As one man explained, he was inspired to do this after listening to the popular hit Thai song with the immortal title *I'm Vasectomized.*

On Sales Pitches, Bad

A prostitute from Florida who had moved to Hawaii was puzzled. Friends had told her that Hawaii was the place to be to pick up wealthy Japanese tourists. But she just wasn't finding many takers. She had learned some Japanese from fellow prostitutes, but potential Japanese customers were either ignoring her or walking the other way.

Only when she had been arrested did she learn the truth from a friendly undercover officer. She had been approaching Japanese men and, in effect, telling them in Japanese such friendly things as "F**k off!", "I've got VD. Wanna have a go?", and "Get the f**k out of here, you dirty asshole."

On Screwups, Hotels and

A Chicago hotel sent thank-you letters to each of twelve hundred former guests for staying there in the past several months.

The problem was they chose the wrong computerized mailing list. The thank-you letter was sent to twelve hundred people who *hadn't* stayed at the hotel.

A harried hotel manager discovered this when the hotel switchboard started lighting up. The hotel was swamped with calls.

One pregnant woman tearfully said her husband didn't believe the baby was his. Instead, he thought it was produced during an illicit stay at the infamous hotel. Hundreds of other spouses called to say now they realized what their opposite number was *really* doing during his/her long lunches or late nights. The harassed hotel manager commented, somewhat dryly: "Husbands and wives don't trust each other much these days."

On Senior Citizen Fund-Raisers, Hot Times at

A local senior citizens' group in Bemidji, Minnesota, was trying to raise money for its building fund. So a public-minded movie theater owner had a great idea—he would turn over two days' revenue from a movie showing.

The owner told the steering committee of the Senior Citizens' Council that, of course, he'd show a family film. But it was a shame, he added, because the *real* draws at the box office were X-rated films.

The committee saw his point.

The Erotic Adventures of Zorro opened at the theater several days later—drawing 170 people, some of them the senior citizens themselves, and earning $825 for the fund.

On Sex and Agribusiness

A farmer in Uganda was sentenced to ten lashes with a stiff cane by the judge. His crime was a bit unusual—abstaining from sex with his wife.

But the man had an excuse: "Commercial reasons." He already had fourteen children by three different wives, and enough was enough. After all, he explained, he was in the process of crop diversification—something all the agricultural experts recommend—and in his words, "The effort needed takes all my strength."

The judge didn't buy this agribusiness line. He ordered the man, after his caning, to spend some time with his wife in "the time-honored way"—plowing the fields, so to speak.

On Sex Changes, Confusing

It was a first for the Putnam County jail.

They had a prisoner who was supposed to be jailed for traffic offenses who was a transsexual—still in the process of changing from man to woman.

Technically, the prisoner was a female from the waist up and still a male from the waist down—pending surgery.

So how did they search him/her for weapons? No problem. The resourceful officers at the jail called in a matron to search the prisoner above the waist. When she was done, they called in deputies to search him below the waist.

On Sex Changes, Surprise

Ramona Cortez's career was going nowhere. So the forty-year-old Bolivian actress did what many aging actresses do: She went in for a face-lift, thinking it would make her feel like a new woman.

But she wound up feeling like a new *man*.

"When I saw Miss Cortez on the operating table, I thought: 'She should be a man!' and I set to work," explained her plastic surgeon to a local newspaper. "I am good. I am quick. I am cheap."

So he gave her a sex change operation.

The upset Cortez immediately did what any actress would: She called her agent, who rushed over to the clinic to comfort her. But once he saw Cortez, he wasn't as angry. In fact, the doctor had been right. Cortez looked great as a man. So the ever-resourceful agent renamed her Don Jeraldo on the spot—and got to work.

It all worked out for the best. Cortez's career finally did rebound. Shortly after becoming a man, she nabbed the part of a fisherman in a popular television series.

On Sex Criminals, Odd

Shanghai, China, was the site for a crime wave—"sex criminals," as the local press called them, were running around sticking sewing needles into young women's rear ends.

No word on whether the culprit or culprits were caught—or, more importantly, why they were doing this in the first place.

On Sex Ed., Nefarious Plots and

St. Paul, Minnesota, was where a social crusader extraordinaire, spoke of the "Sex Education Plot" back in 1969. The key point: Large U.S. corporations and the U.N. were plotting with the commies to destroy U.S. society. How? By offering free sex education classes to children.

During his St. Paul rally, the doctor made several other points. He said that being a homosexual means you do not believe in God. He also offered his somewhat odd argument against nudists:

"If God had meant for us to be nudists, he would have created us with fur."

On Sex Ed., South Carolina Style

Beaufort County, South Carolina, adopted a unique sex education curriculum in 1989. Instead of bothering with a lot of potentially controversial stuff on penises and vaginas, the sex education program focuses on bumper sticker making, with slogans like: CONTROL YOUR URGIN', BE A VIRGIN and DON'T BE A LOUSE, WAIT FOR YOUR SPOUSE.

On Sex, Goats, and Men

A farmer from a small village in Sierra Leone was in court. He was accused of making love to a goat. And his case brought justice to a standstill that day.

When the charge was read aloud in Court No. 1, the accused started laughing and witnesses, court officials, and members of the public also burst into laughter. They couldn't stop–and continued laughing for a good twenty minutes.

The reaction spread throughout the municipal building—first through the neighboring Courts 3 and 5, then on to the steps of the courthouse, finally into the street.

As an official put it: "People could not contain themselves as word of . . . the charge spread. It was not until lunchtime, when hunger intervened, that [everything] calmed down, and by then many other offenders were demanding to be dealt with."

On Sex Guides, Campus

Maybe they were inspired by the success of consumer guides like *Zagat* and *Consumer Reports*. Whatever the reason, two female juniors at MIT (the Massachusetts Institute of Technology) published their own consumer guide in the school newspaper—one with a twist.

Their consumer guide ranked the men's sexual abilities. It rated thirty-six men on campus they had slept with on sexual performance, physical looks, personal hygiene, and so on. The best of the bunch got a four-star rating, others ranked lower, including a few unlucky with zero stars.

School officials suspended the two women—but not before the entire campus read the ratings.

On Sex, High-Flying

Turkish health officials have put out a bulletin warning of an unsafe sex—on rooftops.

Apparently sex on the roof is a big thing during the hot summer nights in Turkey. No problem. But some couples get so hot and heavy they forget exactly where they are—and roll right off the roof.

On Sex, Incompatibility and

A seventy-three-year-old man had just been married to a woman he met at a dating service—a fifty-three-year-old retired cleaning woman.

The happy couple went by train to their honeymoon hotel in the countryside. In the bridal suite, the man, evidently somewhat confused regarding normal procedures during honeymoons, settled down in the bed—and began reading the Bible. Hours of Bible reading passed, until it was 2 A.M. and the man was suddenly interrupted when his wife—now nude—jumped playfully onto the end of the bed.

The man took it the wrong way. Instead of responding appropriately, he hurled his Bible at her. Then, looking about for a means of escape, he jumped out through a nearby window. He landed in a snowdrift. He was followed soon after by his wife, who chased him around in the cold night air for two hours.

Finally they were both apprehended by local police. In jail the man said, "I've had enough of women."

The woman asked for a replacement husband from the dating service.

On Sex with Men in Blue

During an investigation in Memphis, Tennessee, a local woman and mother admitted to having had sex with several hundred policemen.

When asked why, she stated, "It may have had something to do with my belief in law and order."

When curious investigators asked if making love in police squad cars with policemen armed to the hilt with guns, truncheons, sharp badges, and so on, was difficult, she calmly said, "It's just something you have to get used to working around."

On Sex Schedules, Must-Keep

Sergeant Backston of the police received a report of an indecent act taking place on a public vehicle.

When he arrived at the scene, he discovered Stewart Jones making love to Kathy Peterson on the floor of the 15B local bus.

But Jones had an explanation. He was the bus driver. His own car was in the garage for service. And it was Thursday—the night he always had sex. So, since he didn't have his car, he picked up Mrs. Peterson with his bus on the way to the garage.

On Sex U.

A financial officer of the University of Illinois was arrested for spending over $300,000 on prostitutes in the late 1970s and early 1980s.

The finance official was not completely dishonest, however. He charged off the prostitutes to "monthly consulting fees."

On Sexual Prowess, Crime and

A twenty-seven-year-old burglar in Bavaria, Germany, broke into a house only to find it wasn't empty. A thirty-nine-year-old house-wife was there.

Instead of calling the police, the woman told the burglar she'd do nothing if he made love to her. The burglar, sensing a good deal, did just that; and after lovemaking and a drink of water, he was back off into the night.

So he was very surprised when a few days later he was arrested for burgling her house. What had happened? In court he saw the angry housewife. She apparently had decided to prosecute.

But why?

"He may be a good thief," the woman told the court, "but he's a *lousy* lover."

On Sheep, Inflatable

An environmentally aware couple from England saw an ad in the *Daily Telegraph* for rechargeable batteries and sent away for them.

But instead of receiving the batteries, they received an interesting advertising flier in the mail—suggesting that they buy a Luv Ewe—an inflatable sheep, costing only 17 pounds. This, according to the manufacturer, would solve the problem of "how to bring the joy of sheep into your love life without the obvious problems of a real sheep."

The final sales pitch: "No bleating to alert neighbors. No risk of ruining your prize lawn."

In spite of this, the couple decided not to buy—they wanted their rechargeable batteries instead.

On Sheep, Scientific Evidence on the Sexuality of

"Does Lesbianism Exist Among Sheep?"

This was the burning question posed by a graduate student at the University of California in her groundbreaking research project.

But, unfortunately, the question was never actually answered. The reason, as she put it: "If you are a female sheep, what you do to solicit sex is stand still, Maybe there is a female sheep out there really wanting another female, but there's just no way for us to know it."

On Shoplifters

Security guards and police stopped a woman shopping in Falls Church, Virginia, and told her to take off her top at once.

The reason? They were convinced that she had been shoplifting—and had hidden a basketball under her shirt.

But it *wasn't* a basketball.

As the embarrassed security officers discovered, the woman was pregnant.

On Singing Telegrams, Fun

A woman collapsed in hysteria in San Francisco after receiving an unusual surprise singing telegram at work.

Instead of the traditional *Happy Birthday* message, the woman, along with her coworkers, listened in horror as the singer described, in dulcet ones, how great she was at giving head and then elaborated on her other alleged sexual talents. To make the point clear, the singer also waved props around, including a large soap shaped like a penis.

The woman's unhappy boyfriend, who had ordered the telegram as a birthday surprise, insisted he was innocent. He had requested a simple *Happy Birthday* message, he said. The woman decided to sue the telegram company.

On Sink Drains, Penises and

The neighbor of a man in Kennett, Missouri, heard loud shouts coming from his neighbor's house. In a panic, he called the police, who drove over to investigate.

They leaped from the car and, hearing the screams coming from inside, began to batter down the door . . . even though the man started shouting, "Don't bother me! I'm fine! Just go away!"

When the cops got inside, they found the man in his bathroom . . . with his penis stuck inside the sink drain.

It was all very innocent, the man quickly explained. He had been trying to change a lightbulb above the sink—and it just so happened he was nude at the time. Then, oddly, he slipped and fell, somehow catching his penis inside the drain. And when he tried to pull himself out, his penis had swollen so much, he was completely stuck.

Paramedics arrived on scene to give the man a shot that would make the swelling go down—and he was able to free himself without further damage to himself or the sink.

On Smoking and Sex

John Harrison and Zelda Darron were on a crowded London commuter train going from Margate to Victoria when they got the urge to have a little fun. So, in front of their fellow passengers, they had oral sex.

The other commuters watched without comment or complaint.

Then the couple moved on to traditional intercourse. Still no reaction from the other passengers. Once they were done, the two lit up the traditional post-lovemaking cigarettes.

At this point, their fellow passengers got extremely upset and began complaining loudly.

The couple was smoking in a nonsmoking compartment. They wound up getting fined 95 pounds.

On Snow Queens

A beautiful woman, smiling lasciviously, asked a man riding in her truck to take off his clothes and then go out and rub snow all over his nude body.

It sounded exciting. And so, eagerly expecting his sexual reward after doing this, the man duly undressed, went outside, and rubbed snow over his body.

He then looked up from his rubbing—just in time to see the woman calmly driving off with his clothes and wallet.

This was not the woman's first time. Not for nothing do police call her the "snow queen" of Wisconsin.

On Souvenirs, Unexpected

Harriet and Jenny Jimble, two widows in their late seventies, were returning from a pilgrimage to Lourdes, France, when they were stopped by French customs officials. The officials explained that they had reason to believe that the women had certain smuggled items in the trunk of the car.

Even though the women swore they had nothing to hide, the officials searched the car—and, sure enough, found several boxes in the trunk.

The widows didn't know it, but they had fallen victim to a smuggling gang who, to avoid detection, would plant drugs and pornography in the cars of innocent tourists. Unfortunately, the customs officials didn't know it either—and assumed the women were playing coy. So they played a little rough.

As Jenny later told a newspaper: "The customs man started waving what looked like a large rolling pin in my face and shouted, 'Husband no good, eh?' and I replied, 'My husband's dead' and started crying. Then he blew up what I thought was a beach ball and it turned out to be a naked woman with blonde hair. That's when Harriet fainted."

The women were eventually freed without charge.

On Spanking, Vital Questions About

It's not the legal question of the century—but is soliciting a prostitute for spanking the same as soliciting a prostitute for sex?

The question came up when a policewoman posing as a prostitute arrested a forty-year-old Floridian who offered to pay her to let him spank her.

The defendant's lawyer pointed out that spanking is not sex. Spanking is . . . spanking.

The DA's office said that spanking is a form of sex. Spanking is . . . sex.

The judge suggested both sides "research the issue"—although he didn't specify *how*.

On Sports Car Sex

A man and a woman were having sex in the backseat of a small sports car parked across from London's Regent's Park when the man suddenly slipped a disk in his back.

He couldn't move at all—and neither could his girlfriend, who was pinned nude beneath her 200-pound lover.

Desperate to get out of there, she managed to reach over the front seat with her leg and honk the horn. A crowd quickly gathered, all enjoying the free show. Two women volunteers served them hot tea through the window while others worked to free them.

Finally fireman cut away the car frame. The 200-pound lover was lifted out and the sobbing woman was helped out of the car and into a coat. The ambulance driver assured her that the man would be fine—but she was still upset.

"What's worrying me is how I'm going to explain to my husband what's happened to his car," she said.

On Strange Bedfellows

After having a few drinks one night, a man decided it was time to try for a reconciliation with his estranged wife.

She wasn't home when he got to her house, but that didn't stop him. Instead of leaving, he decided he would surprise her. So he undressed and hid in her bedroom closet—where he wound up dozing off as he waited.

When he awakened later, he cracked open the door and realized that she was back—and sleeping soundly in the bed. So he quietly slipped out of the closet and into the bed next to her. His hands wandered caressingly over her body. But something seemed a little strange . . .

At this point, the person in bed woke up with a start.

It wasn't the man's wife. It was her boyfriend.

The boyfriend was furious that another man was feeling him up. And the husband was enraged that there was another man in his wife's bed.

They both leaped out of bed and began brawling. The boyfriend wound up with a broken nose and jaw. The husband was arrested and ended up pleading guilty to doing grievous bodily harm and paying almost $2,500 in fines and compensation. The court also ordered him to perform 160 hours of community service.

But the husband was unrepentant. As he succinctly put it: "What the hell do you expect someone to do when they find a strange man in their wife's bed?"

As for the missing wife—she had been spending the night at a girlfriend's house.

On Streaking

The streaking craze of the mid-1970s—in which people would take off their clothes and run through public places in the nude—was not appreciated by officials in Kenya. They were particularly annoyed by large numbers of Europeans and American tourists who chose to streak in the traditionally minded African country.

So they announced a new—and very effective—law. Any streaker caught by police would be escorted and placed aboard the next available flight home—in the nude.

On Stripping, Embarrassing Moments in

It started out like just another job for stripper Margaret Cooper of England. She was scheduled to perform at a fund-raiser for a local disaster. But it turned out to be a disaster for Cooper.

She arrived at the fund-raiser after it had begun, just as she was told. And she was dressed up as a police officer. When she was given a sign, she jumped out from behind a curtain in full uniform, "arrested" an elderly man, tied him up in his chair, took off his trousers, and began stripping—until all she was wearing was a G-string.

It was then that she realized the man was her grandfather.

On Studs, Overly Conscientious

The owner of Pioneer Emperor Arab, a pedigreed Holstein bull, sued the owner of a herd of cows.

The cows had strayed into the bull's field. Unfortunately, this occurred when the bull was under strict doctor's orders because he was "sexually overtaxed" through his work as a stud. Arab was to do no stud servicing whatsoever for a while.

But the bull was an animal of integrity. When faced with the herd of cows, he did what he had been trained to do. He had sex with all of them.

As one newspaper reported: "Clearly recognizing his duty, Arab nearly worked himself to death."

On Stupidity, Seminude

It happened in Minneapolis in 1972. A young woman who had given birth only a few days earlier got a phone call from someone who claimed to be a doctor. The "doctor" told her that he was following up on recent maternity patients and that she needed to stimulate her milk production by running down the street—he helpfully suggested a street for her—in a T-shirt but no bra. This activity would help her to lactate.

So the naïve woman did just what he said. And when the doctor called her back right after her little jog, she explained that, even though she had done exactly what he said, she didn't seem to be producing any more milk.

No problem, said the doctor. Sometimes the best way to stimulate milk was through becoming extremely *embarrassed.* The best way to provoke embarrassment? She should do the same thing as before, but this time, should cut holes in the T-shirt and expose her breasts.

Okay. Again the woman did as he said. She was as embarrassed as he said she'd be, but nothing else had changed. No more milk. Finally she called the hospital to check up on the doctor's orders—and learned that over twenty other maternity patients had reported getting these strange phone calls.

On Subterranean Sex

The depths of perversion were revealed in Salt Lake City, Utah, where police arrested a man videotaping the bare butts of women.

The man was discovered in an outhouse. Prior to sitting down on the toilet seat, a woman happened to glance into the hole—and saw a man standing waist-deep in sewage, videocamera in hand.

On Swingers

In 1987 a man in Milan, Italy, decided to win back his love the romantic way. He came into her bedroom like an Italian Tarzan, swinging in from a rope attached to a pylon.

Unfortunately, he did it all a little too vigorously. Instead of swinging *to* her bed, he swung *through* her room completely and smashed through the window on the other side, knocking himself out in the process.

All for nothing.

As his girlfriend said, "How could I marry someone so stupid?"

On Swinging Mittens

The owners of the Happy Home Hotel were away on business, but Harold Callanan, a local accountant, helpfully stepped in to run the place while they were away.

All was going fine at the friendly family hotel when a little problem came up. The hotel was supposed to put on a Halloween show for kids and their parents—but the yodeling act that had been booked had just now canceled.

Callanan wasn't too worried. He called a Dublin talent agent, and, on the assurance of the agent, he quickly booked a cute comedy act—the Swinging Mittens.

And so, on Halloween night, in front of a shocked audience of husbands, wives, and children, Callanan's act appeared.

The Swinging Mittens turned out to be four women boxers—who gave a wonderful and innovative show of boxing and tumbles—all topless.

On Teaching Dogs New Tricks

According to the sentencing judge, "By your actions, you have brought ridicule and contempt on yourself. It is very rare indeed to find this offense being committed with the defendant putting himself on the receiving end."

James Mannering of Canterbury, England, hung his head in shame as the verdict was being read. It had all begun several weeks before.

Mannering had returned home from the local pub and, realizing that his two sons were fast asleep in bed and that his wife was still at work, saw an opportunity for a little illicit fun.

Just what kind of fun?

His sons found out several minutes later when they were awakened by the sound of the family dog, an Alsatian named Big Boy (pseud.), yelping excitedly. The two boys rushed downstairs, only to see their father, naked, on hands and knees, with the dog standing behind him with his paws on his back, thrusting vigorously . . .

Mannering, sensing something was amiss, looked up and anxiously explained to his sons that this was all a part of Big Boy's training and to say nothing to their mother.

The boys followed their father's wishes. They didn't tell their mother. But they *did* tell one of their teachers, who told someone else. And pretty soon, the entire town knew all about Mannering's dog tricks.

On Technicalities, Clear

The El Paso, Texas, city fathers passed an antiporno law that required strippers to have certain parts of their body covered at all times.

So the strippers obeyed the law to the letter—and satisfied their customers. It was a clear solution: They covered themselves with clear plastic wrap or Vaseline.

On Technicalities, Transvestites and

Smithtown, New York, police arrested a topless dancer under the very tough laws passed by the city fathers. But they were forced to release the dancer and drop the charges.

It turned out the dancer was a male transvestite undergoing hormone therapy—but still technically a male. And there was nothing on the books about males dancing topless—even if they had large luscious breasts.

An angry local official vowed to further "explore the situation."

On Television Shows, Overly Probing

A Stockholm, Sweden, television talk show gave its viewers what probably is a first in television history: It had a gynecologist perform an actual exam on a woman on the set right in front of the studio audience.

The host said she was "fascinated" by the show—but there's no word on what the audience members thought.

On Testicles, Dollar Value of

A man in Florida lost one of his balls in an accident and was awarded $2,000.

Later Florida legislators in the Florida House of Representatives took up the matter. They agreed that the man's compensation was, to say the least, not fair. "I reckon my balls are worth $200,000 apiece," one politician said. Then the argument turned to which ball was worth more—the right or the left. This matter was unresolved by the hardworking legislators.

One question remained. Why had the jury awarded the man such a low award for such a large—or at least important—loss?

The best probable answer: When the man's case was in court, lawyers referred to the man's "testicles" and jurors probably didn't realize that "testicles" were "balls."

On Thieves, Picky

In 1974 Hartford police were faced with a somewhat puzzling case: There had been a break-in at an adult movie theater, but no one could figure out what had been stolen. The money was still there. The cash register hadn't been broken into. Everything seemed fine.

Then, finally, after careful searching, they discovered the theft:

Someone had gone through every reel of the film *1001 Danish Delights*—and had snipped out and stolen all the nude scenes.

The thief did, however, leave the rest.

On Tight Spots, Penises and

A young man from Inverness, Scotland, had spent the entire night trying to convince his girlfriend to have sex with him. But she kept saying no. The man was getting more and more frustrated. He finally left and went home—about to burst with pent-up sexual energy.

So then he did what anyone might do: He decided to have sex with a milk bottle.

It started out all right—until his penis became too large and swollen and got stuck inside the bottleneck. The man tried to pull it out, but it wouldn't come. Then he tried pulling it out with the aid of butter as a lubricant, but it still didn't work.

He was stuck fast, with a large bottle around his penis.

Then he had a bright, brilliant idea: Why not pour boiling water onto the bottle? After all, hot water causes glass to expand.

He had forgotten, however, one little thing. Boiling water also causes penises to burn—which is what happened. In extreme pain by this point, he finally smashed the bottle.

Said the doctor who wound up examining him: "He presented a bleeding, scalded member, complete with bottleneck still in place, which we had to remove along with all the splintered glass."

On Tollbooth Clerks, Sex in the Slow Lane and

A tollbooth clerk on the Pennsylvania Turnpike was fired from her job, accused of "behavior unbecoming an employee."

Her crime? She had had sex with a truck driver in her tollbooth.

But she was back in her booth a short time later. A legal arbitrator ordered her reinstated—"because the dismissal notice was not specific enough."

On Too Much of a Good Thing, Part I

A Kuwaiti man was thrilled to be marrying his seventeen-year-old bride.

But only a week later the honeymoon was over.

Friends who visited him found him pale, complaining of incredible pain in his back and total exhaustion. Dizzy and disoriented, he collapsed in his living room and had to be carried on the shoulders of his friends to an ambulance.

Doctors weren't sure what was wrong with him until they discovered one crucial fact: His nubile wife and he had been having sex six times a day.

On Too Much of a Good Thing, Part II

A Tennessee truck driver asked for $10 million in damages.

The reason: his defective penile implant.

He claimed to have suffered blisters, bruising, infection, and embarrassment. More specifically, his attorney explained, the man would be "just walking down the street, and it would erect on its own."

On Top Secret Sex

A Japanese government official had a little secret. He liked to visit a video peep show each day after work—without his wife's knowledge. And one day, while he was enjoying his secret hobby, he got the shock of his life. On the screen was his wife—starring in an exciting sex scene with a very well-endowed man.

Not one to take things lying down, the government official did what government officials always do: He launched an official investigation and learned that his wife had a few secrets of her own.

She had been secretly seeing another man. They had been going to a hotel, where hotel clerks had secretly set up a hidden videocamera to videotape their clandestine sex.

And the hotel clerks had been secretly selling these hot sex tapes to the sex shop where the government official had been going after work.

On Tortoises, Sexual Problems of

Monster, a Galápagos tortoise at the Hogle Zoo in Salt Lake City, had been celibate for ten years—and now he was ready for some hot sex with a female tortoise.

But, according to the zoo director, all of Monster's mating attempts were failures. The tortoise was totally inept when it came to sex.

The apparently nearsighted and overeager tortoise had been trying to mate with a rock, a feeding pan, and a garbage pan lid.

The zoo director said they would try to acquire a female Galápagos to help the hapless Monster out of his dilemma.

On Tough Defenses

A man attempted to assault a woman, but found that he had taken on more than he had bargained for.

Not from the woman, but from the woman's pet guinea pig—

which she carried around in her bra. When the man went to rip the woman's bra off, the guinea pig bit him—viciously.

The wounded criminal was apprehended and arrested.

On Train Track Sex

An Ohio man decided to add a little zing to his solo sex act—and tied himself to a railroad track to masturbate.

But he couldn't untie himself quickly enough when he saw a train coming.

The train hit him.

On Trash Disposals, Sexy

A mechanically minded man in Toronto, Canada, took apart the sink in his kitchen and then stuck his penis in the trash disposal unit. After the unit did its grinding and crushing work, he called EMS personnel.

When asked by horrified doctors and nurses why he would stick his penis into a trash disposal unit, he said, "I wanted to see what it felt like."

On Uncle Sherman

In 1976 an enterprising company came out with an Uncle Sherman flasher doll.

The twenty-inch doll came equipped with a trench coat that could be flipped back to reveal a tiny penis and patch of pubic hair made of yarn.

On Under-the-Sink Sex

A newly married couple in Belgrade, Yugoslavia, was having trouble with their sink. Unbeknownst to the wife, the husband called a plumber—who arrived at the house to work on the pipes while the wife was still out. She returned, saw a pair of legs sticking out from under the sink, and assumed it was her husband. She unzipped his pants and, as *The Times* of London delicately put it, "Exactly what she did next is not certain, but it caused the plumber to bang his head into the sink above him." His injuries were serious enough to warrant calling an ambulance. The attendants put him on a stretcher and began carrying him downstairs when one of them asked him just what had happened.

When the plumber told him, the attendant laughed so hard he dropped the stretcher, causing the plumber to fall down the stairs and break his leg.

The plumber wound up in the hospital, threatening to sue. And the wife was so upset by the entire incident that she would have nothing more to do with her husband.

On Unsafe Sex

A British man was having an affair. So he and his girlfriend met in out-of-the-way places to avoid getting caught.

One day the two were kissing and fondling in a deserted area on top of a 220-foot cliff on the Isle of Wight. The woman later explained that they had been lying side by side, but then her boyfriend climbed on top of her—and they were "contemplating having sex."

Unfortunately, they never did get around to it.
The man rolled off the cliff.

On UPS Trucks, Condiments and

Three women from Lansing, Michigan, were arrested for stealing a United Parcel Service truck and taking it for a joyride.

But this wasn't your average joyride. When the women were apprehended by the police, they were nude—and completely covered with mustard.

"It was just a lark," one of them told the cops. But they never explained about the mustard.

On Vaginal Flute Playing, Problems with

If you play the flute with your vagina, you might expect a little trouble. But you wouldn't think you'd have a problem with your choice of music.

But this was just what happened to Miss Amy, a musician from Calgary, Canada, one night. Police were called, according to Detective Jones, after "Miss Amy, who was using her private parts to play *Mary Had a Little Lamb* on a flute, was repeatedly asked to play *Over the Rainbow* by a member of the audience . . ."

And he wouldn't stop. *"Over the Rainbow!"* he kept yelling. *"Over the Rainbow!"*

Finally Miss Amy's husband couldn't take it. He burst from backstage, jumped into the seating area, and tried to throw the heckler out. But in his frenzy, he accidentally hit one of the policemen—and a melee broke out.

On Veg-O-Matics, Dangers of

A Dutch man and his girlfriend were partying together and wound up in his kitchen, drunk and naked.

"For a joke," his girlfriend decided to apply his portable electric vegetable mincer to his groin. A policeman, called to the scene, said, "There was lots of blood everywhere and it looked serious at first glance."

Fortunately, it wasn't, although they both learned a valuable lesson regarding portable electric vegetable mincers.

On Vice Cops, Cost-Conscious

Two Santa Ana, California, vice cops deserve special commendation for performing their duty but also doing their bit to save taxpayer money.

They were supposed to go into a porno house to see what was

going on. And they noticed that admission was $5 a person—but only $8 a couple.

So the cost-aware cops did the right thing to save taxpayer dollars: They held hands, walked up to the door, said they were a couple, and paid the special rate—saving $2.

On Vocalizing, Dangers of

Police in Fulton, New York, received an urgent radio call: Rape in progress. They gunned the motor, raced to the apartment building where the rape was taking place, jumped out, and banged on the door.

No one answered—but the cops could hear movement inside. So they broke through the door and ran inside, guns drawn.

All they found was an embarrassed couple on their honeymoon.

"I do get a little loud when I'm having sex," the new bride explained.

On Weather Reports, Hot

In 1980 the following weather report was transmitted by the National Weather Service:

> *Thursday evening storms produced a massive orgy in southwestern Georgia and northwestern Ohio. Balls the size of hail were observed at Attapulgas, Georgia . . . Elsewhere around the nation, sexually active Americans were indulging in almost every kind of straight sex except for some reports of S&M in California and western Oregon . . . with some heavy whips and chains at higher elevations . . .*

After a long pause, the report concluded:

> *Please disregard the above weather summary, as it is not current.*

It turned out that a new NWS worker was practicing his teletype skills—and had no idea that the machine was connected to the brand-new computerized system.

On Wedding Videos, Unusual

A man and a woman had just gotten married—and like many modern couples, they had paid to have the entire ceremony shot on videotape.

Just after the ceremony, the bride wanted the photographer to find a pretty spot on the church grounds for the final part of the wedding video. The photographer led the wedding party to a grassy area behind the church and began directing the people where to stand. Then suddenly they heard loud grunts coming from the long grass on the side.

As the bride described it: "When we went over to look, we found a nude couple 'bonking' away like mad. Our best man asked them to stop, but they just redoubled their efforts."

It was getting late, so finally the photographer took matters into his own hands.

Said the bride, "He asked me if I would mind them being in the background of the official wedding film. And so they are."

On Wine Tastings

Two friends decided to sample the new Beaujolais nouveau at a new wine bar in the south of England.

But when the owner of the bar, Phillip Jones, poured them a glass, they noticed that the wine had a cloudy look to it.

They called the owner back over. "What's your opinion of this?" Susan Harrow asked him.

Jones didn't give them any opinion at all. Well, not any verbal opinion. Instead, as Harrow later described, "he opened his fly, removed his penis, and popped it into my friend Lisa's glass. Then he handed the glass to his wife, who sipped it and said, 'Delicious.'"

After that, Jones said, "Pay up and get out."

They did.

On Working Professional Sex

A couple, wanting some threesome action, called a well-respected escort service and hired an escort. During a presex beer, the couple explained their ground rules: no anal sex, no same sex action, no intimate kissing, no inside ejaculation. All well and good.

But when it was time for action, the escort couldn't get an erection. He claimed that the ground rules inhibited him; besides, he had already had four other jobs that night. The couple asked for their money back. The escort refused, saying he had done his best.

So the couple shot him.

On Zoos, Porn Needs of

Zookeepers in Japan are concerned. Daiko, a female gorilla, just isn't that interested in sex, frustrating her mate, Sho, as well as the zoo officials, who were hoping for little baby gorillas. The solution? Sex videos—which should stimulate the two into lovemaking. One problem, however. Animal porno isn't that common.

According to the keeper: "If there's a porn video of gorillas, we'd really like to get our hands on it."